MW00937424

Praise for *Anything is Possible*

A Wonderful, inspiring, motivational book! This book is a step by step lifestyle changing road map for a better, more satisfying life. It provides self reflective activities and exceptional insights with real life strategies. This organized, thought provoking first time effort is a delight from Richard Dedor. Richard's own exceptional personal journey is woven throughout. Anyone can use this book to get re-inspired.

Janet Slimak
Program Director of Continuing Education

Richard has put together an excellent resource that's not merely about living your dreams and passions, but also about why and how to do just that. In his short life, he's exemplified what it means to make a difference and dream big, and this book is a testament to that. If you're curious about whether or not anything really is possible, read this book and watch your doubts disappear.

Sam Davidson
Author, *New Day Revolution:*
How to Save the World in 24 Hours

Warning. If you are not a fan of conviction's nagging tug, then don't read Richard's book because his motivational stories, thoughts, and ideas might just change that tug into an action that will change your life.

Adam Nelson
DepositHope.com

Published by Richard Dedor

EAN-13: 978-1-4499289-3-3
ISBN: 1449928935

Library of Congress Control Number: 2009913083

Editors: Stephen Barnes, Karith Humpal and Nathanael Porembka
Page Design: Nathanael Porembka and Richard Dedor
Cover Design: Nathanael Porembka

This title is available for special promotions, premiums, and bulk purchases. For more information, please contact the author at information@richarddedor.com

Printed in the United States of America

Anything is Possible

a book about life, dreams, and believing in yourself

Kitty,

Richard Deats

Always dream

Never quit.

Anything is Possible!

Richard

To everyone who believes anything is possible;

and to the man who first asked me what
I was doing to chase my dreams.

Table of Contents

Introduction

In deciding if I should run for mayor of my hometown of Mason City, Iowa, I was torn between fear and convictions. I constantly feared how running for public office at the tender age of 18 would work out. Would the media respect me? What would happen to my plans for college? How would I pay for the campaign? Would my family support me? I had just graduated from high school, and although voted "Most Likely to Run for Office" in my yearbook, this bordered on crazy! I silently wondered, "Can I win?" I questioned if I would have to put college on hold. I had no idea if I would even have the ability to raise the money needed to run a citywide campaign. Fear aside, conviction tugged at me: I believed that I had ideas worth sharing that could change my community. I had a vision for our city, and this would be my chance to implement them. By choosing to run, my ideas would take center stage and I didn't want to lose this opportunity. I especially wanted to show the teenagers in the community that our voices had value, wielded tremendous power and mostly that we were heard. I knew opportunities like this didn't come along very often and I needed to take advantage of it and stand up for what I believed in.

Election Day arrived and I had no idea if I was going to actually run. Our current mayor, Bill Schickel was running for a higher office and should he win, a special election would decide his replacement. In the two months leading up to Election Day, I had created a plan just in case the opportunity presented itself and I decided to run. I planned out every detail about the announcement and how I would raise money. I voted that morning and by the afternoon, I knew I would run if the mayor won his election. I was going to take my passions and my hope for the community and make my voice heard.

That evening I attended the election night party for Bill. By ten o'clock, Mason City had elected him to the Iowa House of Representatives, and he would resign his post as mayor. I sat there sipping lemonade, surrounded by his wife and daughters, friends and colleagues, and I smiled. I knew. I knew, and I believed! Now, the time had arrived for me to stand up for what I believed in.

Three weeks later in our local mall, with about 40 supporters cheering me on, I announced my candidacy and took my stand. I had known for weeks that I would run. Now everyone knew. I was running for mayor of Mason City, and I intended to win!

My voice reverberated against the steel beams, "Part of that strength comes from you: Citizens. People playing a role in government. Taking a stand. And on this ground I take my stand. [...] It's time for new leaders with a new vision for tomorrow. The time is now."

I smiled.

The slogan for my campaign quickly became: The Time is Now. It was my belief then, as it remains today, that the moment to do something is now. The moment to believe in the impossible is now. When you have a dream, chase it! When you have a vision, build upon it! Nothing can compare to the precious present and to live it now. To live it out loud, standing up for what you believe in. That has always been and remains the dream and quest of life. When we set our eyes on the horizon and stay fixed on our dreams and goals, there is nothing we cannot do!

From that November day in 2002 when I announced my candidacy, I have been living the dream out loud. Losing the election did not deter from the fact that I ran for office at the age of 18! I appeared on national television. I have even made it into Sports Illustrated. Now I am a published writer and professional speaker. I am a graphic designer. I own my own company. And the great thing about it comes from knowing that list only represents the beginning. I say that not to sound proud or egotistical, but because it is all part of a dream that started only a few years ago. Looking back, even I sometimes cannot believe where I am today. Every day people prove to me, just as I am proving to myself right now by writing this book, that "impossible" is nothing more than a word to make us run and believe in the potential of possible.

For the last few years I have been lucky to meet amazing and inspired people as I give speeches and attend events around the country. Everywhere I go I see and hear the same thing: Something holds us back from achieving that which we all know is possible. Somewhere in our hearts we know we can do it. You can feel it deep in your bones, but something holds you back.

I don't have any ten-point plans or self-help guides that pretend to have all the answers. Life is meant to be lived, and not by a diagram or list. This book is about helping you to pull your hands out of your pockets and live again. In order for you to get the most out of this book, you have to embrace the idea that anything is possible. If you do not believe it yet, at least put it in the back of your mind.

Throughout the book there will be space for you to write and reflect on questions related to your personal journey. These questions will encourage you to think about your past endeavors and dreams. However, I will primarily ask you to focus on the future and the potential it holds. Every person in this world has dreams, big or small. It is simply a matter of believing that these dreams can be experienced and fulfilled. It does not matter what obstacles may exist, whether it be children, a full-time job, no car, or age. We have to believe in ourselves. It is, I believe, one of the hardest things in the world to do. Our society teaches us to question ourselves and to find faults and weaknesses. Instead, we need to focus on this truth: I can do anything! That's what we were taught as children and it is my sincere hope that by the end of these nine chapters, you will have the tools and more importantly, the right attitude to jump up and grab every dream and idea you have ever conjured. I can't wait to see what you can do!

I am just an ordinary guy who believes in extraordinary things. I am so ordinary that when I used to go fishing with my grandpa, I felt bad for the worm on the end of the hook and wouldn't put the worm on my hook. I would still fish, but someone else would have to put the worm on for me. If I went fishing today, someone would still have to bait my hook. As a little leaguer, my dad and I practiced in our backyard. We worked on grounders and fielding. Then he decided we needed to work on pop-flies. I was so non-extraordinary when it came to baseball that I ended up with a pretty big bump on my forehead when I completely missed one and my head broke the ball's descent to the Earth. The first bone I ever broke—my pinky toe—was at the ripe age of 20 when running to the bathroom. I tried to fly a kite at age 22 and failed miserably. But I still get up every day believing I can do it. I keep learning. I keep trying. I keep believing that anything is possible and nothing is impossible. I believe in the impossible because I see it and live it every day.

The time is now for you to believe in you.

The time is now for you to stop holding yourself back.

The time is now for you to begin to say, "Anything is Possible."

The journey begins now!

What is Possible?

Before we can reach for the stars, we have to tear apart everything that is already programmed in our minds. The journey begins now.

"THE MORE I LEARN, THE MORE I
REALIZE I DON'T KNOW."

-Albert Einstein

Chapter 1

Examine

"USE WHAT TALENT YOU POSSESS: THE
WOODS WOULD BE VERY SILENT IF NO BIRDS
SANG EXCEPT THOSE WHO SANG THE BEST."

-Henry Van Dyke

There are books and studies and commentators all around who make their lives telling other people how to manage their life. That is not the aim of this book. In fact, it's quite the opposite. My goal is simple: Help you understand yourself so you feel free to go after your dreams. For me personally, in 2008 I was having trouble going after my dreams because I was getting bogged down in lists of things I wanted to do but was never organized enough to chase after them. That's when I stumbled across Michael Hyatt's blog. He is the CEO of Thomas Nelson Publishers and writes about a lot of topics, but he has this extremely helpful planning process that I have taken bits and pieces from and developed my own quarterly personal review process.[1] It really helps me examine where I've been, where I'm at and where I am going. That's what this book will do for you as well.

Attempting the impossible requires you to first examine who and where you are and then look at who and where you want to be. It sounds simple enough, but most people do not even think about looking back. They just go after things without really understanding who they are and why they want the things they do. The United States didn't just get up one morning and send an expedition to the moon. Scientists and engineers and a whole group of exploration-inspired people gathered together to figure out how to make it happen. They wanted to explore our moon because it was the next adventure in human exploration. This book will focus on helping you organize your life to chase after your dreams because you cannot just impulsively go chasing. You have to know what you want and how best to get there. It sounds obvious, but once you begin to *believe* that anything is possible, anything will become possible. Thus we must look at where you have been to truly understand where you want to go.

It is the same in business. How many companies can you think of that are reactionaries? Think of Microsoft's reaction to Apple's iPod. After Apple sold over 150 million iPods (they have since surpassed 200 million) and became a social force, Microsoft jumped in with the Zune. But one problem – they only knew they wanted to be like Apple, but they had no idea what their own dream was or how to get there. Now only a few years later and after plunging sales, the entire Zune line stands far below the iPod. They went after someone else's dream, not their own. Put a little differently, you have all heard the standard analogy for going after a goal: Ready – Aim – Fire. Dreaming occurs during the "ready" stage. Aiming is the planning stage. Fire is where our dreams start to become real. Think of all the businesses that use the Ready – Fire – Aim – Aim – Aim method. Microsoft thought they had a great idea and they fired out a product and kept changing the goal until they hit something with their planning. People are like that too. This book is going to help guide you through the Ready – Aim – Fire method, but not in a step-by-step fashion. Before you can get to where you want to go, you must first evaluate yourself and where you've been (ready stage) so that you can begin to discover where you really want to go (aim stage). Then by the end, the fire stage will be much easier and much more attainable.

BACK TO BASICS

Love him or hate him, Bill Parcells is a great teacher. Throughout his career in football, he has taken absolutely terrible teams and turned them around into champions. As coach of the New York Jets he took the team to a 9-7 record his first season at the helm. When he took over the team, they had a 1-15 record the previous season. His third season at the help he took the team to the AFC Championship game. The team lost a close battle in Denver where they led for the entire first half, but didn't score any points in the second half. In the tunnel, after the game, he gave an interview and was asked where the team goes from there. You could hear his disappointment, but also feel his excitement for the future when he said, "You can't pick up where you left off, you gotta start where you started." Spoken like a true coach. But the lesson rings true for everyone. In sports and in life, you can't pick up where the race ends. If you do, you are liable to not think about why things transpired the way they did and thus you may not learn from the experience. If you don't learn, if you don't take the time to look back on everything you've done on your journey, you are bound to repeat the same mistakes and end up with the same result or maybe even something worse.

Albert Einstein's quote is famous, but it fits perfectly: "The definition of insanity is doing the same thing over and over and expecting different results." With each stumble you have to go back to the beginning and do a true examination of who you are and what you need to change or improve to get a different outcome.

Two examples of making simple changes in life come from my experiences in politics and sports. I could write a whole book about what not to do in a political campaign, with a small section on what to do. Through the experience of running for office, I learned how small things like a phone call can make all the difference. If I ever run again, or advise someone, I now know what I will tell them because of all those lessons I learned from my first campaign.

Likewise, I have gained many lessons from my involvement in tennis. I picked up a racquet for the first time when I was 11. We had a wooden racquet hanging in the garage so one afternoon I went up to the park and started hitting tennis balls against the backboard. I'd played Little League for years, but in tennis I found a sport that would be mine. For the longest time, I tried to be like Andy Roddick and hit serves at 150 mph. It took me years to understand that placement is just as effective, if not more so, than power. My coach always said, "Smarter, not harder."

Sometimes it is a simple change that can be made in one tiny step, like making the phone call to a prospective voter or swinging the racquet just a little bit softer. Sometimes it is drastic and requires you to move to a whole different part of the world. But for right now, it doesn't matter. I just want you to look at you.

Do it. Right now.

REFLECTIONS

What is your best personal quality? Write it down. If you think of more than one, that's great! Write down as many as you want.

I just wanted you to think about who you are. It is important to look at who you are today because if you don't know that, even with a goal in mind, it becomes exponentially more difficult to set the mini-goals in between without an understanding of yourself. Now let's look at it another way:

REFLECTIONS

What do you imagine someone else would say is your best personal quality?

Now, building off the first question, why do you do the things you do in life? What drives you?

I am sure you are wondering why I asked that last question, and the reason is quite simple: Often we don't think about why we do the things we do. I believe the reason is because we are always off to the next thing on our list, not taking the time to think and reflect on the experience we just had. Back in 2008 I had a rollerblading accident but afterwards I didn't want to go the doctor. In very typical male behavior, I wanted to prove I was strong enough to handle it on my own. Little did I know I had two dislocated ribs and a bad case of whiplash—among other things. Question: Why did I respond that way? Answer: Because it is how I was brought up and it is a part of our culture. I also responded in that fashion because I have had similar accidents before and nothing bad had ever happened. It sometimes surprises me how often I see people not reflect back on why they reacted, why they decided, and how they came to this point in their lives. While I still have a lot of work to do, recognizing that I have this in my personality has helped me ask for help when I have needed it since that accident.

I believe because we are so connected to our own fast-paced lives, we hardly have the time to do this kind of examination. The crucial step is to purposefully focus on ourselves and evaluate our own actions and the reasons behind them as it relates to who we want to be and where we want to go.

I hope you're starting to ask yourself a few questions about you. Don't be scared. You are amazing! But that doesn't mean there isn't a lot of work to do. As I have already said, before you can get to your goals, you must understand your own obstacles. The biggest obstacle you face every day is you. Frustrating, isn't it? So why are you your own worst enemy? There are two things that seem to always get in our way: routine and apathy.

We live in such a fast-paced world where once you complete one task and achieve one milestone you have to get to the next one. I don't think we often realize that it's happening, but we're just going through the motions. That is routine. When you feel your life becoming too much like a repeating routine, stop, recognize it and refocus your energy on the positive experience you are living. I believe that there are certain things in my life I can and can't control. I can't control other people, but I can control me. That isn't apathy. It becomes apathy when you start to believe you can't do anything to change your course so you just stay on it because the road is already there. Let me tell you something: You can always change your course.

How did we lose control of our own lives? When did life become synonymous with not living? It wasn't always that way. Look at children. They are completely at ease with themselves, and as such don't need to take time to examine themselves. They are happy to be alive because to them it's a great thing! No bills and just playtime. But as we get older, other people start to have opinions and you start getting into trouble. You might build a grand sand-castle and get a cupcake for your efforts. But then you get another cupcake. Before you know it, you've eaten the whole tray and each time you get a cupcake, you become less and less concerned about how you're getting them. That's the long way of saying: as we age we become apathetic towards ourselves. We get comfortable. We like easy. We like safe. We like the sure bet and the ensuing pay-off.

Children don't have to worry about being fired or getting their next paycheck or getting up in front of a thousand shareholders. They only have to laugh and play and watch cartoons. Even if they fail, they are still loved and nothing in their world changes. As adults, we have pressures from everyone and now there is trust involved, relationships, a 401k and mortgage payments. The list goes on and on. It gets back to being safe. It's easier to be a passenger on the train than the conductor. But remember: it's your life and you need to conduct it and control your path. Where do you want to go?

In many facets of life, we're told to play it safe and not examine alternatives. At every level of football, when a team scores a touchdown, the team has the option of kicking to try and get one point, or running a play to try and score two points. Most times, going for the one-point play is the route chosen. It's simply the most beneficial and the smartest play. The one-point is almost guaranteed. But every so often, the need to go for two points arises.

When I was in high school, a neighboring town's team, the Clear Lake Lions made it to the championship game. It was the end of the game and they had just scored and were now down by one point. The coach called all the players over and asked his players what they wanted to do. Score one point and keep playing or try for two points and win or lose on that one play. Either way, the game end. The players voted to go for two. The players said they hadn't come that far to not go for the win. It worked out for them. They believed in themselves, but more importantly, they asked themselves how they'd gotten to where they are. It wasn't by playing it safe and taking the easy road. Now they have a ring to show for it. Going for two isn't safe, but it is a winner and it is taking control of your own destiny.

COMFORT VS. CHALLENGE

In life we need a solid balance of the two: challenge and comfort. Sometimes we have to take the initiative to challenge ourselves when others can't do it for us.

As a sophomore in high school I signed up for the easy English class. And I mean *easy*. The toughest thing I had to do in class was stay awake during *What's Eating Gilbert Grape*. I had more time to contemplate the meaning of life than I had in study hall. So how much do you think I learned? The answer is not much. I could have gone through the motions and received an easy 'A', but aside from being bored out of my mind, I wasn't learning anything! After getting an 'A' on everything, I can remember deciding that, for my own sake, I needed to have a little challenge. I transferred into the tougher "Honors" English class and was in trouble from day one. This class was not only harder, but actually had students in it that cared about learning. It was a far cry from the class I left where people would come and go as they pleased, taking 15-minute bathroom breaks and turning in Internet copied book reports. This new class required work and thought and analysis of books I had never heard of or would have even thought to read. I was in over my head, but at least I was learning, right? After only two weeks in the class, I had to miss a day for tennis, so I had to take an essay test before the rest of the class on a book we'd read. A few days later the teacher cancelled the test with an uncensored announcement. "Because Richard's essay was so bad, we're going to change course," the teacher said. The class cheered and I was stunned and slightly mortified. It was like being thrown to the bulls and congratulated for my success at the same time. Talk about a rude awakening and a slightly bruised ego. Going from an easy 'A' to cancelling a whole assignment because of my poor writing is a pretty big kick in the shins, but one that over time, I became glad to have received. I bugged that teacher to help me do better the next time—and here I am writing a book. This situation was a time when I needed a challenge and found one.

I also remember a time when I was so comfortable that I did not learn either. My freshman year of college I took a macro-economics class, and the same teacher I had in high school was the teacher. Not only did the subject interest me, but also the first time around it was a totally new concept to me and I hoped the college version of the class would be an extension of the first. Unfortunately, the material wasn't all that different from what I had learned in high school. In this situation, I sought comfort over the challenge, and ultimately didn't learn anything new. The challenge would have been taking the micro-economics class, an entirely new subject with a different teacher, and actually push myself to grow beyond what I knew. Even something that small would have expanded my knowledge, and I still wish today that I had challenged myself. Don't make the same choice to be comfortable. It isn't all it's made out to be. A class may not sound like much, but think how much it can impact your life. I have no idea how taking the micro class could have changed my life, but I can say that I am glad I have learned from not taking it, and I try every day not to choose comfort over challenge. And this is just one example of something pretty small – think how important some of the bigger choices in life can be.

Those are two examples from my life where in one case, I decided it was more important to learn and challenge myself. The other example I just stayed where I was and didn't challenge myself to learn more.

You all have examples in your life where you sought the easy road, and sometimes that really is okay. I admit sometimes I want a break from challenging myself too! Taking time to recharge is important, so while you think about times you may not have taken the path to growth, think about all the examples where you took the challenging one!

What you need to think about now is how you can find the right balance in your life. You need to create the right balance of feeling comfortable and feeling equally challenged. A quick way to find your optimum balance comes from Sam Davidson, the co-founder and President of CoolPeopleCare and author of *New Day Revolution*. He says there are two things you need to do in order to create a great balance, and in turn you will be comfortable and yet still challenged.[2] Sam says to first make your life about life. Sounds simple, I know. You need to find four things in your life that you really enjoy – the things you absolutely cannot live without. These should not be work or school related. These are your "life" things. These reduce your stress. The other thing you need to do is balance the work and school stuff. Sam schedules e-mail time, days to write, days to do business prospecting, and then makes the rest of the time flexible. This allows him feel comfortable with his life and challenged in his work.

REFLECTIONS

What are your four life things?

What do you want to challenge yourself on?

Where would reducing the challenge help you achieve some other goals in your life?

It is only when you focus your energies on the things that matter that you will be able to start to tackle those things that you deem "impossible". That's what this book is all about! I have found through all my travels I meet three types of people. The first person doesn't believe in unbelievable achievements. They are stuck in their rut and don't have a clue how to get out. In the middle are the people who believe it one moment and don't the next. They are torn between the comfort of knowing what is to come and knowing how amazing the challenge could be. And on the opposite side are those who tackle impossible tasks and make them possible. But you and I both know they aren't impossible. Nothing is! I'm going to say it over and over until you believe it, so get used to it: Anything is possible!

Part of the reason we don't challenge ourselves as much as we should is the simple fact that we don't like being alone. We don't like to be the lone wolf. I admire people who take a leap of faith in their own belief in themselves. It takes a great deal of faith not only in yourself but also in others to put yourself in a situation where you might not reach your goal. Sometimes you're not going to make it. Other times, you will. There is one other truth: When you do make it, when you are successful doing something that seemed impossible, you gain more strength and belief to do it again.

I know from experience, it's a lonely stage when not a single person is in your corner. I wasn't the best tennis player in high school and everyone knew it. That wasn't the tough part. My toughest battle came from no one believing I could make a difference on our team. But I'll never forget the match my senior year against a conference rival. Our team had been dominated, top to bottom. But my doubles partner and I were winning our match and we were the last match out. The dual between the teams had already been decided, but we didn't stop fighting. We were the one bright spot on the team that night and through our effort, we earned the respect of our teammates that afternoon. No one had believed in us. It is tough competing when you have little support. It's even tougher when everyone is watching and waiting, almost expecting you to fail.

The tough part for us in the 21st Century is that the pace at which we live can so easily make us forget that achievements worth achieving take time. Here I am less than three years removed from starting this venture into professional speaking, and while I am not yet where I want to be, I am enjoying every minute of the journey. I would love to deliver speeches every day, and I am working towards that, but it takes time. I am extremely passionate about my dream so the perceived lack of total success adds frustration. Much like my life-goal to run a marathon. My body wasn't built for that, but I am training to hopefully do it one day. It will take a lot of time and training to teach my body that running more than four miles is okay! I think people too often forget that it takes time because people everywhere find quick success. Guess what? It doesn't matter what they are achieving!

I mentioned it before, but I lost my election for mayor. In fact, I lost it pretty badly if you look at the numbers. I earned 612 votes (14.1%) while the winner received 2,420 votes (55.6%). Now before you go thinking I really blew the whole thing, I should tell you that there were a total of ten candidates and I did come in third place overall! That's money in a horse race, right? The important thing for me is that I ran and impacted the lives of those 600 people who voted for me and untold others who heard and listened to my ideas and convictions. In the end the important thing wasn't that I'd lost, it was that I had run in the first place. Someone as young as me had never run for office in my community. Impossible obstacle? No. Had any candidate in our community ever had a webpage? No. I'd been talking for years to friends of mine about how important it was to care about things in the community, but if I didn't run, I wouldn't have the credibility to make statements like that. At that moment, I needed to run to prove my words and to make others believe and force them to question themselves and everything they believed. It's knowing the difference between where you are in life and who you want to be in the future.

On a professional level I have many goals, and this book is one of them. Of course I would love end up on the New York Times Bestseller List and many would consider that "winning", but one of my main purposes in writing this book is to grow into who I want to be. I dream of impacting your life in a positive way. Like I said before, it's important that you don't compare yourself or your goals to others. If I compared the success of this book to other books, like where it is on the bestseller list, I will likely never believe I fulfilled my goal. This not only leads me down the wrong path, but it also completely blinds me to the truly important achievements from writing this book – impacting you! The positive changes this book inspires in you, while they will never be on any bestseller list and really can't be measured is my true goal and the way I know I have succeeded with this book. Another benefit to not comparing your goals or successes to others is that you stop finding reasons to doubt yourself. Think how amazing it would be that instead of looking at how others succeed, look at ways you already have and how your own successes can motivate you even further.

I often joke that by running for office at age 18 I peaked too soon. While I may joke, I honestly fear that sometimes. When I see that in myself I try to make it the reason why I push so hard today to improve myself. You can always take negative thoughts and turn them into something positive. That may sound cliché and I don't mean to make it sound easy, but knowing it's possible is a step in the right direction. Remember this is a journey, not a sprint.

Personally, I examine myself as much as possible. First and foremost, I look at where I'm spending my time. I look at the organizations that receive my finite time and energy, whether it's an hour a week or the five per week I now spend as a member of a local business-trade board. I ask myself where I am and where I want to be. The first thing I tell myself is that anything is possible! I am a guy, born in Colorado, raised in Iowa, ran for office at age 18, graduated from college a semester early, gives presentations all across the country and has now written a book! I didn't make a plan for any of that. I just did it. Once I figure out what I want, I make a plan. Before a plan gets made I simply live for my passions.

I said in the introduction that this book isn't about how to set goals or make a detailed plan for your future. This book is only about you, who you are and helping you believe in possible for today and tomorrow! It's about you taking control of your heart, mind, and passion to tear down your own barriers in order to help you achieve the seemingly impossible. Oftentimes it's not other people or the red-tape of the world that get in your way. It's you! But I say that not to make you mad or put you on the defensive, but so that you will take a step back and think about it. What you find might show why examining yourself is vitally important to achieving the impossible.

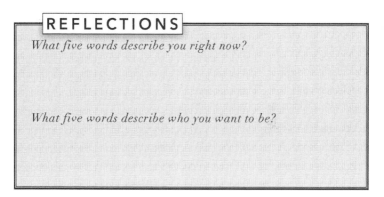

REFLECTIONS

What five words describe you right now?

What five words describe who you want to be?

These two lists are very different. The first one focuses on this very moment. As I have said, you have to know who you are in order to figure out where you want to go. The second list draws attentions to the task at hand: getting to where you want to go. So now the questions is: with the potential difference in the two lists, what makes us push ourselves?

EXAMINE YOURSELF

Think about the people who created the great pyramids. In a world with no cranes to help lift the rocks and stone, why did they do it? As much as the how fascinates me, but the why intrigues me even more. Have you thought about it that way before? Why did they build the pyramids? Why was Stonehenge built? Why carve four faces into the side of the mountain? Why fly solo across the ocean? Simple: Someone either deemed the task impossible or someone just didn't believe it was possible. I may be over simplifying it, and maybe historical achievements are more than acts of just wanting to do something. But that is the point! We all want to do things and for some reason, we all too often tell ourselves it can't be done!

Throughout civilization, humanity has pushed to do things never thought possible, constantly proving "anything is possible!" From Amelia Earhart and Barack Obama, to Bill Gates and Howard Shultz, each accomplishment is a testament to the theory that behind this book. What do they have that you think you don't? In a word: Nothing! What they do posses is the attitude that anything is possible, and then they went out and made it happen. Each time we achieve the impossible, with each moment we see that we can indeed achieve great things, our minds begin to wonder, "What else can I do?" It's a powerful moment when that occurs.

The downside can be that when you falter, the sense of failing and of pure impossibility can easily prevail and we start to slip away to believing that everything is impossible. In moments of failure, your mind has a million different thoughts streaming through it: What happened? What could I have done differently? Did I do the math wrong? Could I have put in five more minutes of effort?

Are you beginning to see that this battle to achieving great things, even impossible things occurs in your head? It's all in your attitude and how you approach your journey.

Others Will Tear You Down

I've lost enough tennis matches to know the feeling of being a total loser. In my early playing days I once double-faulted an entire game. For those you of unfamiliar tennis, that means I served eight times and eight times I missed. My opponent didn't even have to touch the ball. I would have had a better chance of winning a point had I never even served! I have had days where I never thought I would win another match. Losing makes having confidence tough, and it's even tougher when there is already too little within.

My lack of confidence in tennis began at the start of my freshman season in high school. A few days after the season began a few of my teammates made fun of my cheap Wal-Mart tennis racquet. In all honestly, I didn't realize it was cheap. To me my racquet was amazing, and aside from making me feel like a pretty big loser, those jabs also spurred me to do some research. If my racquet made it impossible for me to win, I needed to make a change. Eventually I bought a better racquet, and you know what, I played better! Today I know the difference between racquets, and I pay a lot of time and attention to having the proper tools for the game. But that feeling of being less-than-good dogged me for my four years of high school tennis.

I didn't reach my full playing potential until I was 21, and I don't blame anyone but myself. I allowed their comments affect my attitude. I let that negativity stop me for a long time. Looking back I didn't do enough to change that attitude or change where I was to get to where I wanted to be. It become impossible to me only because I let others lead me to think I couldn't do it. In the end, no one deserves the blame but me. I came to understand that the power to change that attitude, and ultimately the outcome, is not in someone else's hands either; it's entirely in yours!

So, Build Yourself Up

With the larger campaign for mayor, I still believe to this day, that I was also the most passionate candidate. I know that even if people didn't vote for me, my passion resonated. The field contained nine other candidates and I was by far the youngest candidate. When I entered the race, I entered with the understanding that I might lose. However, I always focused on getting my message out and ultimately winning. It was important to focus on how to win, but throughout the campaign I remained true to my overall mission of sharing my ideas and getting the citizens to believe in something new. My focus remained on the doing as opposed to the destination. Losing the election doesn't matter today, the fact that I ran does. That in and of itself is a huge accomplishment.

Think about the people around you. What types of people inspire you? The mopey, complaining, stagnant ones who aren't enjoying their journey and pushing to achieve crazy awesome goals? Or do you find energy from people who believe in achieving the impossible dream while reaching for the stars? Passionate people choose to believe in the potential of life because it is already in their nature to believe in their passions. It's already a part of their thinking and dreaming.

One constant throughout my campaign was the question about my age. The press started this idea that I was too young and experiences and it was a hard viewpoint to turn around. When they weren't asking me, they asked someone on the street. How do you feel about his age? Is he too young? Does he have the experience? My performances in the debates should have proved that my age was irrelevant. I held my own, and I demonstrated the ability to discuss the issues and challenge the status quo. I see now that I made one of the biggest mistakes of my campaign: I let the media's viewpoint get to me. I didn't start to believe they were right but I wondered if I could break through that barrier and therefore I let that barrier keep me back.

The similarity between my high school tennis career and my campaign is that it was never me talking down to myself, at least at first. It was only after others talked down and gave their negative opinions that I started to talk down to myself. What is possible? Anything! But you absolutely, positively cannot let yourself be that barrier. The difference between success and failure was nothing but attitude. I not only allowed others to talk down to me and make me believe things weren't possible, but I also let them start to become a part of my own thoughts as well. Once these thoughts gain root in your mind they can be hard to remove. You may not be able to stop people from saying what they want, but you can stop those thoughts from gaining a foothold in your mind. When you hear them, make sure that's where they stop. I do believe we are our own hardest critic, but we can also be our biggest advocate by keeping the "impossible" attitude out of our thoughts. If it is my own personal thought, then it's just one voice and is easier to overcome and stop. It becomes an even larger problem when others think it and start talking down. Then it becomes easy to start to think it too, and suddenly it does seem like you can't achieve whatever you'd set your mind on.

How many times in life have you let others decide for you what was possible and not? How many times in life have you talked yourself out of a goal or a dream you really wanted to accomplish? I know from countless moments in my life that dreams and goals always seem impossible at some point and the bigger they are the harder they are to get, but the more amazing they are to achieve! What could you have changed? Only you can answer that question. You must before you can go forward. But I bet that nine times out of ten, the answer could come down to one thing: Attitude!

It's a tough world out there and you simply can't be your own worst enemy. It's true on the tennis court, true in politics, true in the classroom, and true at home. Whatever happens, you're the best thing you've got! Believe in yourself and your dream, and at the end of the day — live it!

I still take moments to examine myself and where I want to go. I hope you begin to do so as well! Looking back on who you are and where you've been is a process that never ends. You should constantly look at yourself and your attitude and make sure it remains positive and strong as it can be. The sad fact of life is that there will always be people who think you can't do something or who believe a challenge is impossible. Don't listen! If you believe it, if you have the right attitude and you know who you are, anything is possible!

Points to Remember

» Attempting the impossible requires you to first
  examine who you are and then and only then can you
  look at who you want to be.

» "The definition of insanity is doing the same thing
  over and over and expecting different results."
  -Albert Einstein

» You must understand what obstacles you are up
  against, from yourself and others, before you can even
  know what you need to tear down.

» Seek challenging situations to push yourself but also
  seek the comfortable ones that still challenge you in
  small ways.

» There are always going to be people who will try to
  tear you down.

» Continue to believe that anything is possible to keep
  the naysayers at bay which will keep your positive
  energy up.

Chapter 2

Eliminate Not

As you move through this book, I want you to keep one of your childhood dreams in mind. Don't worry, there is no test at the end, and I won't even ask you to go do it (which is probably a good thing if you dreamed of being an astronaut like I did)! I promise I won't ask you to chase after that specific dream, but it is important to be mindful of what this dream represents: your willingness and ability to dream freely. As you learn more about yourself throughout this book, dreaming freely will become even more important.

In the introduction to this section, I said that in order for you to reach for the stars you must tear down what is already programmed in your minds. Here are a few phrases I believe we've all mentioned to ourselves at one point or another.

I can't do it.

I don't have the tools.

I don't know the right people.

I don't have the skills.

I won't have the time.

I can't make a difference.

Each of those phrases has something in common: It uses the word "not." It may seem like just another three-letter word, but when you use the word "not" you do nothing but limit yourself! You have set up a barrier and the more you say and think it, the harder it is to overcome.

Think about how different it is if someone else sets up the barrier for you. We often let others tell us what our limitations are even if we don't think they exist. But soon outside opinions can manifest themselves into becoming *your* limitations. When that happens, you have given away the one thing you will always control: your attitude. One of the world's foremost writers on leadership, John C. Maxwell, has even written a book about this simple idea of attitude and how important it is to individual success. He refers to attitude as "the difference maker." It is no surprise that this is also the title of his book.

Maxwell writes, "The little difference is attitude. The big difference is whether it is positive or negative." That's what this chapter is about! It's about making your attitude the thing that makes all the difference as you chase your dreams; dreams that become possible when your attitude is right.

You can get over other people not believing in your dreams, but if you internally don't believe, that's exponentially more difficult to overcome. You can only try to change their opinions through your actions and your attitude. What you can do very easily, is change your own behavior – your own thought process.

To put it bluntly, it's your attitude, silly!

WATCH HOW YOU TALK TO YOURSELF

Winning our mock election in eighth grade to become Mayor of Room 228, I began to garner an interesting in government and politics. Soon after that victory, I announced to my family in a bold, confident, and thoroughly clueless fashion that in about 18 years I was going to run for president of the United States (I'm eligible in 2020, so look out for me!). My dad immediately struck me down saying that it would be next-to-impossible for a kid from Iowa to become president. At that moment I became enamored with learning everything I could about politics and American government. I believed it was not only possible, but that I, Richard Dedor, could do it! Only four years later I took the first step towards that dream in my first political campaign. It wasn't the presidential race, but I ran for office. Coming in third in my race for mayor made me realize how hard my dream of the Oval Office would be to achieve, but more importantly showed me I had reason to believe it was possible. Placing third validated that I was indeed right to run and that I had something valuable to give. I didn't allow a negative attitude to take me away from something I was passionate about.

I know my dad was just trying to be realistic, but I was dreaming and that means reaching far beyond what others, and sometimes even ourselves, believe is possible. Dreaming is absolutely what outside the box thinking was designed for. I truly believe that is the nature of dreaming. Michelangelo said, "The greater danger for most of us lies not in setting our aim too high and falling short; but in setting our aim too low, and achieving our mark." For most of his formidable years, Michelangelo was criticized for how much he dreamed of working with marble. His fellow artists, his friends and even his own family said he should focus on something other than art and marble. But throughout his life, Michelangelo dreamt of marble night and day. Staying true to his passion and believe in himself explains why he is regarded as one of the world's greatest artists. Never mind that his works have stood the test of time and still bring people from all over the world to view his creations.

Think about that. Dream not just big, but the audacious! Soon after the mayoral campaign, I let myself lose that dream. It became an afterthought. I'd let losing the race cloud my passions. I let the voters dictate my attitude. But then one day while reading political news and getting excited about serving my country again, I decided I wanted to re-claim my dream. I was no longer going to tell myself that my political aspirations were not possible. I'm now back to discussing issues and learning as much as I can, so I will be ready when I'm called to run again. It's fun to think about: Richard Dedor, President of the United States. Possible? Absolutely!

Let's get back to the point about you talking down to you. Who places the most limitations on you? Where does most of your negativity come from? The answer is that it probably comes from you! Surprised? It usually is ourselves that talk down to us the most. It is us that says we can't do something, be something or achieve something. An article published in the *Australian Journal of Early Childhood* reports that children as young as three understand that they are having emotional feelings and thoughts, but are just beginning to understand what they mean and how their emotions were triggered. At this early age, the researcher points out; childhood is seen "as a time of powerful and active involvement with the world."[1] What this says to me is that children are not only open to it but are willing to experience every emotion that comes with human exploration.

We are taught growing up that we can do, be, and achieve anything we set our minds to. But something along the way has changed for adults. This coincides with the previous research in reporting that children are more open to experiencing their emotions and believe they are in control of their own destiny. But as children turn into adults, that sense of personal control seems to dissipate.

Since you can't get away from yourself and if it is you stopping you, the solution lies in changing your attitude and how you talk to yourself. *Have you ever tried running away from your thoughts only to find them right beside you the whole time?* Think about how many things you hold yourself back from doing – all the negativity or downers that make you believe you can't do something. Sometimes you may search for an excuse not take a risk. Your mind is powerful and imagine how amazing your life could be if you turned those thoughts into something positive and empowering. That is a huge part of our goal. No matter if you are a high school or a 50-something, we can all improve our ability to think positively.

When I ran for mayor, I had the full support of my family and friends. Without them the road would have been a lot bumpier. Our lives become easier when you have a strong support network. But sometimes all you need is belief in yourself. It doesn't come easy and there are bound to be bumps in the road. Andre Agassi, a retired eight-time Grand Slam singles champion and Olympic gold medalist said in his retirement speech:

The scoreboard said I lost today but what the scoreboard doesn't
say is what it is that I have found. And over the last 21 years I
have found loyalty. You have pulled for me on the court and
also in life. I have found inspiration. You have willed me to succeed sometimes even in my lowest moments. And I have found
generosity. You have given me your shoulders to stand on to reach
for my dreams. Dreams I could have never reached without you.
Over the last 21 years I have found you and I will take you and
the memory of you with me for the rest of my life.

Agassi started out his professional career on fire but then for a period of about six years, he under achieved. In the middle of his career,
his opponents were not the ones beating him. Yes he needed others' belief too, but he needed his own more! He was beating himself. He was
pushing himself to lose, to not be focused on his goals. He fell so far as
to use hard drugs for a year when he was at his lowest point. It was only
when he was virtually the only one in his corner did he start to re-focus
on his dreams and goals. Of course, I'm not suggesting you abandon
your support network to go after your dreams. What I am getting at
is how important it is to remain focused on your attitude, otherwise,
nothing else matters. Through it all, Agassi's fans were loyal and always
pushed him to win.

While tennis remains a huge part of my life my career isn't as dec-
orated as Agassi's, Federer's or even the 1,000th ranked player in the
world. But what my tennis career does have posses is dedication to the
game and a true belief in self and of my own abilities. I was made fun
of my first season of high school tennis because I played with a rather
cheap racquet. At the time, I thought I was pretty good, but I found
out had a long way to go. It took that realization to make me want to
work harder and improve my skills so that I could have a better chance
at achieving my goals. I struggled throughout my high school career
because I not only let others' attitudes towards me affect my play, but I
also didn't have much belief in my abilities. After the racquet incident,
I told myself I wasn't good enough. Belief in my abilities didn't happen

until I had played for over 10 years when I finally figured out how to win: eliminate "not" from my attitude towards my tennis skills.

I had played tennis scared for a decade. It's over simplistic, but I was scared to be good. I was scared to work hard enough because I didn't believe in myself. The more I played and the more I lost, the more I began to beat up on myself for losing and having a negative attitude. About a year after my high school career ended, I began to understand my attitude and how important it was to my lack of success on the court. I immediately changed and began to focus on the aspects of tennis I was skilled at and I found that once I started hitting the ball and driving through my shots, I saw I was hitting better, playing smarter and enjoying myself more. Did it amount to more wins? You bet! Did I still lose? Absolutely. The most valuable thing I gained had nothing to do with a record; I found belief in myself and an inner strength that makes all the difference in the world. This has impacted not just my tennis game, but every aspect of my life from working out to starting my own company.

The problem is when you defeat your own ambitions, you already lose and the opponent or the obstacle you are facing has an easy victory. The biggest reason that happens is that you tell yourself that the small things don't matter – that you can let a negative attitude win the little battles. *But if you give them that power, how can you expect to overcome them for the bigger things?* So often you can get into that bad groove, and it only gets harder and harder to get out of the next time. By not defeating your own ambitions and dreams you allow yourself to win those small battles that come along every day. By winning these small mental struggles, you will build up a resistance to the negative thoughts that come into your head. The key to winning the struggle against yourself is to be conscious of it. When you hear the negative thoughts in your head, stop them!

I am a firm believer in the power of positive thinking and the Law of Attraction. As a tennis player, I am an easy study in how powerful our thoughts are when it comes to attraction. For any athlete, having a negative thought pop into their head, increases the likelihood that the negative thought will become a reality. It wasn't until late in my tennis career I began to understand it. I still struggle with this problem on the court, but I've improved through my mistakes. When I hear the negative thoughts, I take a pause and refocus my energies and thoughts. Sometimes refocusing takes two seconds and sometimes it takes ten minutes of bad points. The important thing is to remember to listen to yourself and stop those thoughts from becoming routine and a dream stopper.

When Barack Obama announced he was running for President in February 2007, almost no one gave him a chance. Not the pundits and not even his own party. But from the very beginning and dating back to his days at Harvard, he believed in himself. He not only believed in himself, his message, and his dream – but he made it happen. Over the next 21 months, America and the world saw what belief in one's own vision can do. We saw the change that can occur simply from having a positive attitude. His attitude first empowered him to move forward. Then, those close to him supported his ideals, then a campaign, and then an entire nation.

REFLECTIONS

Think about something you always wanted to do, but never did. Write it down here:

Now answer the following question: Why didn't you do it?

Everyone said Senator Obama was too young. Instead of allowing the "age" problem be the story, he used it to his advantage. Almost every presidential campaign that I've followed, each candidate says they will change Washington because they have all these new, innovative ideas. Like him or not, Obama said just that. He said he was new and would offer that "real" change. For him, age became a positive attribute because he wasn't seen as a Washington insider. The electorate ended up not only looking past his age but they never made it an issue. Of course his opponents did, but it never worked.

Pundits doubted his ability to raise enough money to defeat, let alone compete against the Clinton campaign machine. Then suddenly in March 2008, Obama raised nearly double the $20 million raised by the Clinton campaign. That margin would continue to grow throughout the rest of the campaign. The numbers themselves are staggering, but it was done with such incredible ease. I believe part of the reason for his incredible success is because of his strong persona (a.k.a. his attitude). By the end of his two years of campaigning, Obama raised a whopping $744 million,[2] the most in history by a wide margin. (In his 2004 re-election campaign, then President George W. Bush only raised $269 million.) Even up until Election Day there people said Obama didn't know enough and didn't have enough experience. The simple fact is that he believed in himself and he slowly made other people believe in him as well. There were countless times during the campaign when he could have succumbed to negative press, but each time he managed to turn the story around. That's how powerful his attitude towards his abilities was. Without it, people would have questioned his age and his ideas more. But because Obama had a strong conviction about his abilities, the electorate never saw a reason to not trust and believe in his message. Now he is the President of the United States and his vision has remained the same.

NO EXCUSES, GET TO IT

For me, one thing I've always wanted to do is ride RAGRAI, an annual bike-ride across the state of Iowa. I lived in Iowa for 18 years and each your I had many excuses for why I didn't ride. While I didn't have the equipment (which isn't hard to get at all), I never researched other options. It was me stopping me. My current excuse is that I don't live there, which while still a terrible excuse, I say it because I am putting my energies into training to run a marathon, not ride a bike across Iowa. I will ride RAGBRAI someday.

Sometimes it is okay to tell yourself no. As a child I dreamed of being a famous performer. All the fame, movie deals, performing for thousands of adoring fans before a quick autograph session was my vision. It is still something awesome to think about! I definitely did not give enough thought to the importance of being born with or developing the talent. You can always become talented through practice (and more practice), but that takes work and a personal belief. For me, it was just a fun dream since I didn't have the passion. Without the practice and passion, it is a good idea for my own sake and everyone else's that it remained a dream ... unless of course I am alone in my car and then I am totally on tour!

Growing up and sometimes event today I think I'd make a great actor. Finally, my senior year of high school I decided to give it an official go with my debut as the Captain in *The Marvelous Playbill* by Tim Kelly. My speech coach asked me to fill the roll and I gladly accepted even though I had other speech obligations at the time. It was a tremendous challenge to act in a play for the first time, but the other actors helped me through the learning process. It remains one of the highlights of my high school days. I did something I never thought I'd do and now I look forward to the day when I do it again. Notice how I didn't say, "I hope I can do it again"? My attitude is that I *will* perform on stage again.

Why stop yourself in your tracks before you even get started when the thrill of chasing is so great? It is time to stop acting as your own worst enemy.

IF OTHERS TALK YOU DOWN - DON'T LISTEN

Now that I have you thinking about how you talk to yourself ... what about others? How do others talk to you? But more importantly, do you listen? I'll be the first to say that it's often hard not to listen, but by being aware, we can take a step towards freedom from others' negativity.

The first question to think about: *Why do people talk down to others?* There are many words for it and you've heard them all: pessimism, skepticism, cynicism, doubtful, gloomy, naysayer … you may even be able to apply those words to some people around you. These words breed equally negative attitudes and come to life when an idea is looked upon as less-than possible, too hard, too dreamy or, my personal favorite: a personal far-fetched dream. But the great thing is if I'm dreaming it – if I'm able to think it – then it is in fact *possible*!

We listen because it is an integral part of being human. Face it, we like to hear people's opinions and get approval from our family and friends. From the moment we are born we seek approval and praise from others. We tend to want attention and more often than not it can be tempting to settle for negative attention than none at all. Life is not like publicity, and not all attention and talk has a good effect on us.

Children display this need for affirmation by doing an art project and then revel in the pleasure of seeing mom and dad put it up on the refrigerator. Teenagers do it by doing well on a test and getting a bump in their allowance or scoring the game-winning touchdown to win praise from their teammates and coaches. Young professionals do it by creating new and trendy ways to do business and earning a promotion. Some adults do it by purchasing the most expensive car so they can show it off around town. We continually and constantly seek the approval of others.

There are two truths about our search for approval. First, there is nothing wrong with seeking approval. Oftentimes this approval helps us know if we are on the right track or need to adjust our trajectory. Second, it is a fact of life that we seek approval and it is not going to change. The important thing to be mindful of is how the approval or lack of approval we receive from others affects us.

The simple solution is nothing more than listening to comments, positive or negative, see what we can take from them and move forward towards your goal. Sometimes your goal changes based on the approval or lack thereof, but you can't simply let the absence of someone's approval stop your dreams. There are of course times when you will need to completely change your plans simply because the lack of approval is correct. But maybe it will serve as motivation to get you working towards your vision even harder.

Medical student, philanthropist and my best friend Asitha Jayawardena, serves as a great example of not giving up on a dream. I can honestly say I have never seen him quit just because someone else tells him: No, impossible. During his junior year of college at Gustavus Adolphus College, Asitha volunteered to serve as co-chairman of Building Bridges, a group on campus that hosts a diversity conference every spring. In 2008 the group chose "Genocide Awareness" as the theme of the conference. As planning progressed, Asitha wanted to find a way to have the conference attendees prepare meals to be sent overseas to refugee camps in countries where genocide was occurring. He first called the United Nations and was rebuffed. He tried a few more avenues, calling numerous non-profits in the area. He persisted in continuing to call the U.N. with more questions and ideas, but was repeatedly turned down. Finally, he found an organization in Minneapolis whose primary mission is a larger scale version of his vision – to provide meals to refugees all across the globe. This organization fully embraced Asitha's idea, and proved to be a valuable partner that helped make the project a success. In one day, Asitha and the conference attendees packed over 40,000 meals for refugees around the world. *40,000!* After being told his efforts were a waste of time, he not only fulfilled his personal vision, but directly impacted thousands of people. My point is this: don't let others talk you down! Not only can you find a way to succeed, but the rewards often extend far beyond just yourself. If you still believe even without their approval, then eliminate "not" and find a way!

My sister Tracie is also another great inspiration to me. In June of 2000 she was on an eight-week long mission trip in Slovakia. This trip was an opportunity for her to work with all her passions. Since attending Concordia University in Seward, Neb., she had grown leaps and bounds in her desire to spread Christianity and this trip would give her a real taste of work in that arena. For as long as I'd known her, teaching was her purpose in life. I can recall warm summer days where I would have rather wanted to be outside playing with my younger brother, but Tracie would have us down in the basement, giving a lesson on math.

She even had the stand-up chalkboard to teach us lessons and called on me and my brother to come to the board to work out problems.

Teaching in Eastern Europe was a far cry from the basement lessons I'd endured years before. That fall she was starting her super-senior year of college and had never before been out of the country. Her job was to teach English to students at a Lutheran high school in Tisovec, Slovakia. With two weeks to go, she went with some of her students on a hike during one of her days off. The destination was a nearby mountain, and although it wasn't large, it was rocky and my sister wasn't skilled or trained in hiking of any kind. While climbing back down the mountain she slipped, falling about 45 feet, breaking both of her legs as well as other minor injuries. Air-lifted to a nearby hospital, the doctors refused to release her for travel back to the United States for two weeks. Despite their best efforts and intentions, medical treatments in Slovakia were antiquated and downright scary next the quality of care we are used to here in the United States.

Finally, upon arrival at our local hospital after two weeks of mediocre treatment, doctors told her that because of the care she received overseas, they would try their best, but walking again without pain and without struggles was going to be a long-shot. I was there when Tracie heard her diagnosis, and I'll never forget that, "Oh, no you didn't just say that because you don't know me," look in my sister's eyes. I knew then that I was going to make sure that she would overcome this. I was there every step of the way, through all the physical therapy sessions at the hospital and at home. I was there offering encouragement and holding her hand. I was there when she wanted to stop trying and accept defeat. But through it all, she never let herself quit and never gave in to the doubt. It was probably the hardest thing she had gone through up to that point, and the struggle lasted for months after the accident. Even today she'll experience pain in her leg that contains the rod and screws.

Once rehab began, she had two goals: walking and being on campus and in class for the first day of classes. In that order. She wasn't going to let herself down, and she was certainly not going to let her dream of becoming a teacher down. There was always a part of me and my parents that wondered if she would achieve either of those. The doctors actually tried to talk her out of going to school. She didn't consider it. She went. Even though she was still using a wheelchair, she was there the first day of school. That was what mattered to her. A few weeks after the start of the semester, she was on her feet – walking. She not only proved doctors, friends, and even some family that she could do what they thought impossible, she proved it to herself. Like Asitha's vision of helping so many others, my sister's determination has touched the lives of each of her students, and has inspired countless others, including me. She said she would when they said she couldn't. Better yet, she went on and did it! It was never easy, but it was as simple as that "no" she kept saying to all the "don'ts" and "can'ts," even when some must have come from her own tired legs and mind.

REFLECTIONS

When did you have a goal or a dream that no one believed you could accomplish and what was that dream?

How did it make you feel?

What was the outcome?

BACK TO YOUR ATTITUDE

If the outcome wasn't what you wanted, ask yourself what you could have done differently. *Did you say no to the negativity?* What would have been the key to success that you needed? (I'll give you a hint … just asking for something to be easier is never the answer!) If you did achieve the outcome you sought, then ask yourself what aided your success. Truth be told, you're going to face challenges like that again.

You're going to have a dream or a goal and someone will try to talk you down. Someone will say it can't be done. It's how you respond in that moment, when the battle is between "is" and "not," "can" and "can't," ideas of what is possible and impossible. You must choose to believe in *is*, *can* and *possible*.

At the same time, if someone isn't saying it can't be done, or someone isn't saying 'don't,' maybe you aren't dreaming big enough. Maybe there are even bigger and greater things for which you can reach, and even bigger goals that you can achieve. When you dream the impossible, don't just settle for what you already think is possible. Dream huge big audacious dreams! As John C. Maxwell writes in his book, *Put Your Dreams to the Test*, "Dreams, by definition, are not supposed to start with reality. They are supposed to be fantastic, incredible, and out of the box."

When I became an assistant coach of my high school tennis team in 2004, I had the great fortune of being surrounded by a very diverse group of athletes. The team itself was made up of skilled players and passionate athletes. Some played just to play. Others played just to fit in. Some played because they were really good. The people who are most passionate typically are the most successful.

One player on that team epitomized everything this book is about. Tylor Schlader, then a senior from a nearby town (30 miles away), went to a school that didn't have a boys' tennis team. He battled with his athletic director and ours to get the chance to play because he was passionate and competitive. At first they told him no because of rules and regulations, but he didn't quit pushing and asking for the chance to play. It was in his fight just to have the opportunity to play for us that Tylor began to cultivate his drive to succeed and willingness and almost near necessity to always fight for every point. Finally, they relented and let him play for us. This is a case where it was important to keep pushing for approval to get the opportunity to chase dreams. But the story gets better.

He struggled in his first match as a varsity tennis player. I remember before the match he was visibly nervous. As an athlete, you never want to show nervousness because opponents usually try to capitalize on it. Tylor wasn't that way. Even when he was down, he never beat himself. Opponents had to always beat him. He fought hard in that first match, and what I saw on the court has never left my mind. I saw a kid grow up right before my eyes and start to believe in not only his talent but his attitude. He lost the match and afterwards as we talked about it, he mentioned he wanted to throw up most of the match because he had been that nervous. I have to admire a guy who allows his emotions to challenge his passion. He quickly became our top player and it was because in that one match, he saw and began to believe and understand that if his attitude was in the right, winning would come naturally.

He improved so much that year that he decided to play college tennis. He started out at Loras College, but the school just didn't fit him quite right, so he transferred to the University of Iowa where he wasn't even given the chance to walk-on to their team. Never defeated, he transferred a third time to Wartburg College. There he found his home and honed his skills. He worked his way to the top of the team and became one of the most respected players in the conference. He never became a conference champion, but everyone knew him and no one wanted to play him! The thing about Tylor is that he never quits – on any point – ever. He reminds me a lot of Rafael Nadal in that respect. Having played him countless times over the years, I know it. I can hit an amazing shot that 75 percent of my opponents won't ever return, but against him, I hit it and it comes right back at me. I know from coaching him and playing with him that it's not usually a killer shot, extra hours in the gym or even natural born talent. It's his entire attitude, his passion, determination and sheer will, and I love every minute I get to spend with him on the court.

The best thing is that this 'never quit, never say never" attitude positively flows into whoever is around him. That type of attitude is contagious! He has carried that persistence and passion with him into his professional life as well, where he continues to drive, continues to push towards his dream without ever succumbing to the belief that things are impossible.

CAN, WILL, HAVE

I hope by now you are beginning to understand how important it is to believe in yourself and not let others talk you down. As you start to challenge yourselves to greater heights you also have to keep a watchful eye on the vocabulary you use to talk to yourself. It should always be: I can. I will. I have. This seems simple, but it's crucial to your success and overall happiness.

A few years ago, I was fortunate enough to meet Marty Stanley at a seminar. Marty drew on over 25 years of experience as a human resource and organizational development executive in developing a concept she called, "Get out of BED." Through her research, she found that when people eliminate the blame and excuses and stopped feeding off of denial, they began to find more success in their jobs and their lives. Only when we eliminate those bad words of can't and won't, can we truly believe in possible. Those three words: blame, excuses and denial, are paramount to those who don't believe their dreams are possible. For in the end, it is all up to you to make things possible in your life.

I mentioned before that as a tennis player it took me awhile to realize how to be successful on the court. It was never more evident than at the 2006 Iowa Games. A qualifying event for the State Games of America, and in the first match I had to play a Division III tennis player. He hit bigger than me. He seemed to move effortlessly on the court. He even warmed up with ear buds in, almost mocking me in the sense that here I was completely focused and he was jamming out to his tunes.

As we neared the end of the warm up I started to feel overwhelmed, almost to the point where I knew there was no possible way I could beat this guy. I could feel my heart rate rising and the tensions building up in my muscles. Then I remembered how hard I had worked in the weeks leading up to this event. I remembered that I could play well when I remained positive and stayed focused. I remembered the goals I had worked so hard to achieve, and decided in that moment I wasn't going to let today or anyone else stop me from chasing after them. I certainly wasn't going to tell myself it wasn't possible. That day, I played the best match of my life. In a three-setter, I defeated a guy who on paper and by all expectations was better than me – and both of us knew it. When the final point was mine, I jogged to the net to shake hands with my opponent. He quickly walked off the court; He'd been beaten by someone who believed more in the possible than the obvious final picture we'd both seen when the match began: a quick defeat.

Everyone knew the Packers would beat the Broncos in Super Bowl XXXII. Everyone knew that Dewey defeated Truman. Everyone knew that the world was flat. Only to find out that the Broncos stunned the sports world, that Truman actually won re-election and that when you get to the end of the world, you just keep going on to another adventure. Only when we dare to dream, dare to believe that anything is possible, do our minds open up to what truly is within our grasp!

Points to Remember

» Sometimes we let others tell us what our own limitations are. When that happens, we've given away the one thing we must always control: Our Attitude.

» Only when we eliminate those bad words of "can't" and "won't", can you truly achieve everything you dream possible.

» Aside from others, it is usually ourselves that talk down to us the most.

» There are no good excuses, so get to it!

» You can always take a step away from negativity towards personal freedom.

Possible is Everything!

Obviously not everything is possible because some people can't see color, but that doesn't mean they can't paint. Some people can't read music, but that doesn't mean they can't sing (contrary to what is said on *American Idol*). Some people don't have depth perception, but that doesn't mean they can't still enjoy everything in life.

This section, *Possible is Everything*, could be a book all on its own, but I've boiled it down into three things I believe you need to examine and change to set you on a course to being able to have the attitude that anything is possible. These are real stories and real people, just like you, who even when times were tough with their backs against the wall, kept a positive attitude, continued to live their lives and never stopped experiencing life and its wonderful glories. They believed in the possible, not the impossible.

You can make a difference.

You will challenge yourself.

You have the ability to change your life and in turn, the world.

"IS ENTHUSIASM IMPORTANT IN SELLING? YES, GENUINE, HEARTFELT ENTHUSIASM IS ONE OF THE MOST POTENT FACTORS OF SUCCESS IN ALMOST ANY UNDERTAKING."

-Dale Carnegie

Chapter 3

Prognosis: Positive

"KEEP AWAY FROM PEOPLE WHO BELITTLE
OUR AMBITIONS. SMALL PEOPLE ALWAYS DO
THAT, BUT THE REALLY GREAT MAKE YOU FEEL
THAT YOU, TOO, CAN BECOME GREAT."

-Mark Twain

I've already asked you to look at yourself and who you are as a person. Step one is understanding who you are and where you want to go. Next, you looked at one simple thing you can do to change everything in your life: Eliminate the word 'not' from your vocabulary. I know it sounds too simple—but that's because it is.

The next three chapters will dive into changing your attitude and outlook on everyday tasks and daily actions. As humans we are constantly growing and changing and hopefully that change is toward positive personal growth. Through my own experiences and watching other successful people have the right attitudes, I believe there are three actions you can take, right now, to start changing your outlook on life. These steps will allow you to build the framework for the final section of the book where I will offer up four *dares* for you.

Think back to the last time you walked down the street and you smiled, just smiled for no real reason. I honestly try to do it everyday. Of course, some days are easier than others. Sometimes it is the weather or a child playing that makes me smile. Other times it is a phone call from a friend and sometimes it is as simple as doing something I am passionate about.

You could have a bad day at the office and of course that makes it hard to smile when you leave. You arrive home and you are still upset and your kids see that face and feel your tension immediately. I was told once to leave work at work and enjoy life at home. It is great advice but I know it's hard to follow. Think of what home life could be like if you could find a way to be positive when you walk into the house.

If you have kids, think about what your children feel when you come home upset over something at work. If you don't have kids or want to think of it differently, think of how having a bad attitude affects your cube-mate, your office manager or your mail carrier. Your attitude affects everyone around you and can negatively affect their day. Conversely, a positive attitude can have a positive effect on those around you as well. Your face and your attitude are the most important things at the moment anyone is in your presence.

Let's first look at steps you can take to make this a reality: keeping a positive attitude through the tough moments.

SEE THE POTENTIAL

Keeping a positive attitude allows you to always see the potential, believe in the seemingly impossible, challenge the unchallengeable and see doors that are covered by negativity.

When I lost the election for mayor, I could have been glum and angry that the citizens didn't look past my age or inexperience to cast their vote for me. I lost to someone who raised more money than me and who was much better known than me in the community. I could have blamed the loss on my age. I could have blamed it on my inexperience. I could have done that. I was certainly surprise by the outcome. The entire week leading up to the election I got the sense that our campaign would have a very good showing.

Placing third in a field of ten candidates and garnering 14.1 percent of the votes really solidified my belief that running for office had been the right thing to do. The positive side of me thought we would win and the negative side thought I would be lucky to even get the votes of my friends and family. Of course that is extreme, but in a political campaign anything really is possible. When Bob Johnson, my former teacher and campaign advisor, handed me the vote totals, I shook his hand, thanked him for his council and then made my way to give my concession speech. I was surprised by the margin of victory for sure, but also humbled by the percentage of votes I received. I had prepared two sets of notes: One if I lost and one if I won. The funny thing is, they both were virtually the same. Celebrating a victory is easy and of course I would have preferred to give that speech. But I believe the true character of a person is demonstrated in how they respond in defeat. I thanked my supporters and congratulated my opponent. I finished by reminding everyone that even though the votes didn't go our way, we were victorious in raising issues. We got new people involved in the political process. We inspired the community to care, listen and debate real issues for the first time in recent memory. For all those reasons, I won.

Who would have been the real winner if I had gone out and showed anger and disappointment? I kept a positive attitude because I really believed, and still do that my campaign was successful. Of course I was disappointed the election didn't turn out my way! For the next month I struggled with the fact I had lost. I analyzed what I had done to lose and what I could have done to win. Regardless, I am still proud of my effort. Losses are tough, but I bounced back. It's now a story I love to tell. Even today I'll receive a random email or Twitter message from someone who remembers when I ran. Telling the story of how I ran and not focusing on the loss keeps the positive part of the story at the forefront. It's what people remember and what I love talking about. My third place finish proves that anything is possible for those who have a passion and believe in their vision. My campaign proves that if you stay positive, the hard work will pay off. Equally important though, you can't listen to the naysayers because you can achieve anything you put your mind and heart into. Running for office actually started my speaking career. Shortly after the election, I was hired to speak at a meeting of the Worth County (Iowa) Republican Women. When I spoke at their luncheon, I had no idea it would take me where I am today, but anything is possible!

When I attended the 2001 LCMS (Lutheran Church – Missouri Synod) Youth Gathering in New Orleans, not only did I experience to a culture different than mine back home in Iowa, but I was also greeted with amazing messages based on inspiration and hope. It is no surprise that a city built below sea level that the theme for this gathering was *Higher Ground*. Throughout the week, the theme demonstrated that with hope and faith, we too can reach *Higher Ground*. While this was a religious event, I took the messages of hope and turned them into life lessons on how I should approach my life and the importance of remaining positive through all situations.

One of the speakers, Tom Rogers, a pastor from New Orleans, greeted our roaring crowd of 30,000 teenagers with a chant that quickly began to reverberate through the entire lower bowl of the SuperDome and all the way to the rafters. Rogers explained to us that for years, the fans of the NFL's New Orleans Saints had endured countless losing seasons. In fact, after the team began in 1967, the team didn't have a winning season until 1979 (they went 8-8 that year). They didn't have another winning season again until 1983 (another 8-8 season) and lightning didn't strike again until 1987 (when they went 12-3). Talk about needing some uppers! Rogers, a lifelong Saints fan shared that since the beginning; Saints fans were passionate and devoted and never let their depressing yet consistent losing record get them down. Since 1967, Saints fans have chanted, "Who dat? Who dat? Who dat saying gunna beat our Saints?" Ironically everyone beat them! But say what you will – stupid optimism or blind hope – they always believed their team had the potential to be great. This has surely made those precious few wins even sweeter, and worth every single chant!

Now use that chant for you. "Who dat? Who dat? Who dat saying gunna take your attitude?" Only you get to control what your attitude is. For Saints fans, even with losing season after losing season, the fans remained positive. I can't go back and count, but I know I have lost more tennis matches than I have won. But I still believe I can win every time I go onto the court.

THE POWER OF ATTITUDE

As much as I believe in the power of a positive attitude for you, I also believe the power that positive thoughts and words can have on those around you goes largely untapped. *How many times do you hear positive words coming from those around you?* Conversely, the power of negative thoughts and words, whether your own or from others, is a personal killer, stalking you every step of your journey. It kills your goals and your aspirations dead in their tracks.

Let's go back to the Saints for a moment. Imagine if the team said in 1967 that they weren't going to have a true winning season until 1987, 20 years after their debut. The only people in the stands for those years would have been families, friends and people who had nothing else to do. Let's look at my campaign. If had come out in my first speech and said to everyone listening that I probably wasn't going to win, how likely would I be to get the votes needed to win let alone compete? How could people even believe I was passionate about my vision? Your attitude will not only have an effect on you, but everyone around you. Make your attitude something worth catching and grabbing onto.

REFLECTIONS

Think of every great idea you've had and why they never came to fruition. Pick one of your ideas; write it down and why it never saw the light of day:

Now think of a great idea you've had and why it did become a reality. What was it and why did it come to life:

Chances are the first reason you listed was that someone didn't like it, didn't believe in you, thought it was too expensive, didn't have the time or they simply just didn't believe it was possible. Or maybe it was you saying it wasn't possible. This translates into a negative attitude towards the idea, towards the potential that lies within every challenge. My guess is the idea that came to life was because you or someone else believed in the possible and had a great attitude towards achieving it. When you have a positive attitude and believe in something, you are more likely to be successful no matter what the dream.

A great example of the power of positive thought is athletics. You would be amazed at the infinite examples how incredible the power of positive thought is for athletes. It's absolutely true that athletic success is 10 percent muscle and 90 percent effort. That effort is comprised of passion, determination, patience, attitude, and of course, that crazy thing – positive thinking. As a tennis player, I am a true advocate in the power of belief in one's own abilities. If you think you can, you will. If you think you can't, you won't. It's true with trains and it's true in life, business and sports.

As a tennis player and with anything in life, I like to win. Actually, I love it! I love the thrill of the victory and hate the agony of defeat, but it is all part of the game. The need for skills aside, athletics require a belief in your personal abilities. It probably comes as no surprise to those that know me, but I'm not the best tennis player, or the best athlete. But I do know one thing: I work hard at the things I am passionate about so when I am in competition, even if my opponent is better than me, my heart, my passion, my work and my overall positive attitude of being the best I can be is what will carry me through. I don't just mean a belief in your athletic ability but also a belief that when you are losing; you can still come back and win. Again, this is not just measured by winning and losing. Of course it has an impact on your view of success, but maintaining a positive attitude can help you through the tough moments of competition.

Anytime I miss a first serve, one of two thoughts goes through my head: *just put the damn serve in* or *don't double fault.*

Which train of thought do you think is more likely going to lead to success? I'm speaking from experience that when I think the second one, *don't double fault,* 90 percent of the time, a double fault will result. And no, I am not just a bad tennis player! Your mind and your body are connected in ways we'll never fully understand, but I do believe that if you think it, the probability of your thought coming true is higher than if you don't think it.

One of the greatest tennis players ever to play in my opinion is American Andre Agassi. I admire him not only for his record on the court but his passion and drive off of it as well. As he neared the end of his tennis career, he and his wife, tennis great Steffi Graf, set up the Andre Agassi College Preparatory Academy in Las Vegas. It's a modest yet successful school where the goal is to offer academic programs designed to enhance a child's character and to instill respect, motivation and self-discipline. In fact, the school doesn't offer any individual sports teams because, according to Agassi, it goes against the mission of the school. The second half of Agassi's tennis career was molded around character, respect, motivation and self-discipline. But his character and gentleman-like demeanor on the court and his hours in the gym late in his career, pushing himself to stay on top of his game makes him a champion in my book.

He will be remembered by the sports historians as a player who played his heart out and when he wasn't on the court, he was working on his physical fitness, ensuring that when the moment came, he would be ready. In the twilight of his career he was hampered by sciatica caused by two bulging discs in his back, a spondylolisthesis (vertebral displacement) and a bone spur that interfered with the nerve, causing him great pain and limited his ability on the court. But his attitude never changed. Whatever people are thinking on the inside, it usually shows on the outside. I could never see that in Agassi. "The great part about tennis is you can't run out the clock. As long as we were still playing, I have a chance," Agassi said. No matter what the score, he always believed he had a chance and you could see it in his body and in his eyes. He was always in the match. That is why it was great to watch a player like Agassi play, because you always knew there was a chance he could come back. People, no matter if they are athletes or writers, teachers or singers, as long as there is a positive attitude and belief, you still have a chance.

NFL quarterback and future Hall of Famer, Brett Favre is a perfect example of trusting one's abilities. Love him or hate him, the guy can flat out play. He has often been called a "gun-slinger" for the way he plays the game. He has always trusted his abilities, even as the end of his career neared. When it comes to where to throw the ball, he has never gone for the easy check-down or dump-off play. He goes for the home-run, the laser-tight spiral into triple coverage. He isn't always successful and I'm sure he drives his coaches nuts, but he trusts his arm and more times than not, he finds success.

Is it coincidence that he has a positive attitude and enjoys the game at age 40 the same way he did when he was 18? I think not. He believes he can do it and his teammates feed off that attitude. That's what I enjoy so much about him – his ability to make something happen out of nothing where other quarterbacks would throw the ball away or even go so far as to question their own abilities. He is the ultimate competitor who always believes he can do it, no matter the circumstances. His three Most Valuable Player awards are one of many indicators that speak to his attitude about his abilities.

A better way to look at Favre is the number of records he owns. In 1997, he became the third (Payton Manning became the fourth in 2008) player to win the Associated Press MVP three times. He led the Green Bay Packers to seven division championships, four NFC Championship Games, two NFC Championships and one Super Bowl championship (XXXI). He holds every valuable NFL passing record: most career touchdown passes, most career passing yards, most career pass completions, most career pass attempts and most consecutive starts among quarterbacks. The argument can be made that Agassi and Favre and hundreds of other world-class athletes are just flat-out talented, but how many other hundreds upon hundreds of others have tried to make it but didn't? Of course, some of those were in fact because of talent, but others are quite simply because of a bad attitude and absolutely no level of talent can overcome a negative attitude.

Now look at a guy with a poor attitude: Ryan Leaf. He doesn't have many statistics because his career was marked by injuries, poor media relations, and ultimately poor performance. He is widely regarded as one of the biggest flops in NFL and professional sports history. It was his attitude about the game and how to handle his fame that aided his fall from the NFL.

REFLECTIONS

Is your attitude worth catching? What small things can you do to improve your attitude?

Outside of athletics, this concept of having a keeping a positive attitude works in business, school and life. The most successful business people are the ones who maintain a positive outlook and believe that with the right information and the right attitude, anything is possible. A poor, negative attitude doesn't exist for them. The list of names is long: Warren Buffet, Donald Trump and Hillary Clinton are but a few. They have achieved great things because they believe in their abilities and will try anything and everything to achieve success. It all begins with attitude.

During the credit crisis and ensuing recession in the fall of 2008, Buffet didn't panic and sell off his holdings. Instead he continued to invest his money and personal fortune back into the economy in a show of faith. That's putting your money where your mouth is. If you spend any time reading about Trump's business deals and aspirations, you'll see that rarely does he take no as the final answer. When he decides the vision in his head is worth going after, he's going to do everything in his power to make it happen. Clinton was First Lady when she ran for the United States Senate from New York state in 2000. When she ran for president in 2008, she was in her second term as senator and became the first woman to be a major player in a presidential election. Those three people couldn't have made it as far as they have without an attitude inside themselves where they believe anything is possible. With the right information, the right training, and ultimately the right attitude, you too can achieve anything. It's not a Hallmark card, but it is simple and vitally important to remember and believe.

Attitude not only affects your life, it impacts everyone around you. It was this understanding that Ron Clark used as a teacher in an inner-city school in New York City. Clark used special rules, innovative teaching methods and had an immeasurable devotion to his students and their success. He went so far as to search the neighborhood for one of his students who had stopped coming to class. He took his entire class to a Broadway showing of *Phantom of the Opera*. He also worked through a terrible bout of pneumonia. But he never quit. Not even when the students rebelled against him and his optimism. Clark's attitude slowly started to catch on. From day one, Clark believed in the potential of the perennial underachieving students. With each failure, he worked to teach the lessons of potential and opportunity. As the students started to learn, they started to believe in themselves. In the end, Mr. Clark's class earned the highest average in the state on the state exams. Clark worked to change his students' attitudes and in the end, they achieved more than even they imagined.

YOUR ATTITUDE IS YOURS, AND ONLY YOURS

Not everything in life depends solely on you, your abilities and your attitude. I suspect everyone has a love/hate relationship with group work. Groups and teams can be refreshing because the task load isn't as big and the successes and failures aren't all on your shoulders. Sometimes there is even the chance to slack off and let that A-type go-getter person do most of the work (not that you or I would ever do that)! Then again, groups can really be terrible because you have to rely on others and you no longer control the outcome all by yourself. Working in groups doesn't end when high school and college ends. Odds are that you will work on various team and groups your whole life. I can attest to the fact that it is sometimes excruciating to have our success rest on someone else's work, especially when you may not get along in the first place.

Naturally, it happens that there is one person who not only wants to give 120 percent, but also insists that you do too. On the other hand there is at least one person in each group who would rather clip their nails than do their fair share of the duties. And of course there is you who is absolutely normal and just so very excited to be a part of this fun called group work!

Group dynamics like that are normal and something we must get used to. It's all too easy to sink into a negative attitude towards that person that wants us there at 6:30 a.m., and even easier to get angry at the one that eats all the donuts and never brings any! In a simplistic form, it is all too easy to detest group work completely. The problem is that negative attitudes not only weigh you down, it weighs on the group, and just amplifies a problem that you could actually solve easily with an adjustment in your own attitude. While it may seem unfair to expect that you do the work to compensate for someone else's attitude and performance, adjusting to the environment and those around us is really a normal part of everyday life. We just don't like to when we feel we are being made to make up for poor attitudes by that A-type or non-worker-type. Instead of being frustrated, try and catch some of that drive from Mr. 120 percent. Or even better, be determined to not be the one who doesn't pull their weight. Not only will this elevate your attitude, but you get a much better result for the whole group as well!

While it may seem like the un-luck of the draw, there are many people out there who have poor attitudes and you will work with them at some point. You may feel they suck the life out of you, and there will be days where you just want to throw in the towel. Sometimes, just cutting your losses and finding a new situation and a new attitude is the right move. Other times that isn't an option and you must find a way to cope in order to keep your mind in the right place for success.

REFLECTIONS

What person or group has the biggest positive impact on your life and attitude?

Conversely, what person or group has the biggest negative impact on your life and attitude?

What can you to do limit the effect of the negative attitudes that are around you?

I wish I had a three-step plan to help you change your attitude. Unfortunately, I don't. I only have these stories of real people finding and keeping a positive attitude, and the results of that attitude. If it is your job that hurts your attitude, maybe it's time to ask for a transfer, go back to school to find your true passion, or find a completely new job elsewhere. Nothing is worth remaining unhappy for. Perhaps a vacation or just a day free of thinking will help.

My best advice is to remember that it isn't about you. When someone has a negative attitude and is stuck in the *that's impossible* or *that's too hard*, mode, it isn't about you. They are fighting a battle or they may feel they have already lost and simply can't find their way back to the light of believing in possibility. It may not even mean they have a "can't" attitude. By simply not pulling their weight, not wanting to do the work or not being passionate about the project, it hurts the teams' ability to stay positive and be successful. Whether it is someone else dragging your attitude down or you feel like you're slipping into negative mode, you can change it.

There is a simple tool I've developed that I have shared with audeinces since 2007. It's called 'My Best Times List.' The concept is simple and you've probably decoded that cryptic title already! It is a list you create and keep with you. Post where you need it most: on your refrigerator, your bulletin board or in your desk drawer. The card is filled with positive moments and memories that invoke an image that recreates your positive energy from those memories. Reflecting on your positive memories is a very simple positive reinforcement tool that you pull out at any time to read, take a few deep breaths and remember those great moments. Just like rebooting your computer, the card helps you reset yourself back to zero and gets your attitude to focus on the positives in your life. You might even find a smile creeping onto your face! Imagine what that would do for your day and how wonderful it would be when you're ready to punch a wall. Instead of negativity and anger, you can think back to your best golf game ever, a beach far away or the birth of your child, and remember how many amazing reasons you have to smile! A simple moment like that can take you through any day and any challenge.

At the end of this chapter is a completely blank page for you to create your own list. Tear it out if you'd like and use it however you want! Place it somewhere where you can get to it quickly should the need arise for a restart. If you're like me, you might even want to make a couple for different locations depending on what stresses you have in your life. I've even gone so far as to write the world "Believe" and "Possible" on the toes of my tennis shoes just as a quick reminder for me during a tennis match. When I am on the court, it always helps to remember that I did defeat a Division III tennis player in the 2006 Iowa Games. Yes, I can do it! And it's a great thing to smile about too.

I believe if you have a positive attitude and you surround yourself with people who also have a positive attitude and limit your exposure to those who don't, you will be more able and more apt to go after those things which seem impossible.

Points to Remember

» Your attitude affects everyone and everything around you.

» A positive attitude now may seem like a waste of time, but the results will come.

» You get to decide every moment of every day what your attitude is going to be.

» The power of positive thought is immeasurable, but you can sure tell the power of a negative thought.

» Surround yourself with those people and groups that promote a positive attitude in you and the other people involved.

Chapter 4

Live

I'll never forget the first day of biology class in tenth-grade. I entered the sun-filled science lab excited because I was in Mr. Friday's class and he was the "cool" science teacher and since science wasn't my favorite nor was it even close to my best subject, I was excited to have this guy as my teacher. He didn't disappoint. The first day included the typical explanation of class rules and assigning of books, but then he started his first lesson. His passion for biology quickly filled the room. He started the discussion off by leading a discussion about what science was to us and what we enjoyed about it. We finished with another discussion on the etymology of the word *biology*. By the end, Mr. Friday was in the front of the room saying, "… it's the study of life!" I was hooked. Life is amazing and beautiful and it is meant to be lived. Mr. Friday is the perfect example of someone who knows their passion, isn't afraid to show it and never quits.

WHAT IT MEANS TO LIVE

The largest audience I have ever spoken in front of was that of the family and friends gathered at my high school graduation. It is a story that I love to tell, not only because of the speech itself but for the obstacles beforehand. As one of two speakers chosen after an audition process open to all seniors to speak at our commencement, I was told how to dress, all the way down to my shoes.

My graduation party had been the day before and I had stood on my feet the whole afternoon in a pair of new dress shoes. My feet were tired and sore and I didn't want to go another afternoon of wearing dress shoes for hours. I thought I could bend the rules a little bit. Normally I tend to follow the rules and it's not that I wanted to break them just for the sake of defying authority. I simply wanted to be comfortable and wear my brand new pair of sneakers. I arrived when I was supposed to, dressed up with dress pants, shirt and tie, red gown with my cap and speech in hand. And of course, my shiny white sneakers. As the processional and ceremony and neared, we all started to line up; myself, the other speaker and the student body president. We stood at the front of the line as we would lead the class out. I was more nervous about my speech than my shoes. I had made it this far so I figured nothing bad would happen.

My sly attempt failed and I was caught with my sneakers twenty minutes before I was to take the stage. Our team of principals didn't catch me. No no … it was my fellow speaker who said, pointing at my shoes, "Where are your shoes?" Our principal looked at me and asked the same question. Standing next to her was the assistant principal who had spoken to all the seniors about our dress code for the event. They both had a look on their face which I read to say, 'You're not getting on the podium with those shoes.' I started to run through my options. I knew my dad had dress shoes on, but I didn't think I would be able to find him in a sea of 1,200 people. I decided my best course of action was to hurry home. A normal trip from the school to my house would take fifteen minutes. I had to make it there and back in twenty. I sped the whole way home to get my dress shoes and return before the processional began. As I was racing down a city street at upwards of 50 miles per hour, I was thinking of just stopping at a stranger's house, offering my wallet as collateral for a pair of shoes for an hour. Instead I kept my foot on the gas. My heart was racing. I'd worked for hours writing my speech and many more hours practicing it and now I wasn't going to get to give it just because I wore the wrong pair of shoes! I reached home, ran inside, grabbed the shoes and got back into the car. Speeding back, I tried to put the shoes on and succeeded in getting on just one. As I pulled into the school parking lot, I was elated I had made it in time. I ran up to the back door of the gymnasium and pulled on the handle. Locked! I couldn't make this story up if I tried. Luckily, a classmate noticed and let me in. The rest, as they say, is history. I made it. I gave the speech. Ironically, my dad can be heard on the video tape noticing my change of shoes, saying, "He changed his shoes."

The message I gave to my fellow graduates that day reflected on a Ralph Waldo Emerson quote, "The creation of a thousand forests is in one acorn." I urged my classmates that no matter what your goals in life are, no matter your road blocks, or how long it may take, to leave the school and go "take root". That's what this chapter is all about! You: taking root and living!

Taking root in your dreams is a total shift in attitude. I said to my classmates that while we have dreams, it may take years for them to come to fruition. All I'm talking about here is simply having a passion, having a goal and going after it. That is living.

So what does my pair of shoes have to do with living? Quite simply it means living your own life, bumps and wrong clothing included. Living means not always letting someone else tell you how to dress and how to act or what your potential is. No matter what, you must live your life as you dream.

My sister is a perfect example with what she did back in 2000. Everyone told her that not only could she not make it to the start of school, but that she would not make it to school at all that year and shouldn't push herself to get back on her feet so quickly. But nothing discouraged her. She eliminated "not" from her vocabulary and as the summer quickly turned to fall, there she was, watching us load up the car for her trip back to school. She'd made it.

Years later, she and her daughter fell victim to the "once-in-a-lifetime" flood in 2008. Living in Cedar Rapids, Iowa, the waters of the Cedar River began to rise. She and her daughter were told to just stay put and they would be fine, the water wouldn't reach them. Twenty four hours later, it was declared a state emergency and she and my niece had new orders to be out by nightfall. As the sun set, the waters they were told weren't coming, came. Never before had the town seen water rise that high or that fast and with no end in sight. My sister and her daughter were able to get out, but she left nearly 29 years of her life behind. Our family all watched on television and online while the waters kept moving into the city. When the waters receded and the city allowed her to return to her home a week later, she had no idea what to expect. She found that her life as she knew it had been entirely washed away. Everything. Every piece of furniture, priceless photos, clothes and stuffed animals, everything was gone or ruined. Whatever hadn't washed away was covered in mud and sewage.

Of course it wasn't easy for her, her daughter or our family. It remained a challenge for awhile, and it is still hard for her to think about it. But after taking the summer to settle her emotions and to find a new place to live, she trekked back to Cedar Rapids ready to start her family's life over. Luckily she had been renting when the flood came, although she was searching for a house to buy prior to the flood. She searched and searched for the perfect house and in late July, just two months after the flood, she purchased her first home and started to settle back into life. Not only was Tracie buying her first house after she lost everything from her last one, but she was living again.

Through the hiking accident she remained positive. Through the flood she remained steadfast in life. In both situations, there were moments where she was ready to throw in the towel. We all get that way. But I want to impress upon you that even with the potential loss of physical mobility and the actual loss of 95 percent of her possessions, my sister chose to live. She chose to pick up the pieces and rebuild her world. Twice.

My sister's stories demonstrate the perseverance required to eliminate *not* from our lives and the important of living our lives with the deck we are all handed. Her story is an inspiration for me to keep moving forward through all my tough moments and to remain focused on living 100 percent of my days.

The former head coach of the men's basketball team at North Carolina State University, Jim Valvano demonstrated the epitome of living life when it was being stolen away. Jim was a guy who worked his whole life just for a chance at glory. He finally found it in his No. 6 seeded team in 1983 when they defeated the University of Houston for the title. Their run to the title remains one of the most improbable champions in the history of college basketball. After his team won the title, Jim was running all around the court seemingly looking for someone to hug and celebrate with. In a moment of complete joy, of reaching the college basketball mountaintop, Jim was overjoyed – as he should be! He'd worked his whole life to reach this moment. *But what if he hadn't won the title in 1983, or any other year in his career? Would his life and the way he lived it be any less significant?*

Years later after that astounding victory, Jim became afflicted with cancer. His condition was terminal. What still amazes me is that despite being in the midst of losing his fight over his body, he vowed to help others who would follow him into that battle. Cancer was taking away his body and life. What it didn't do is take away his ability to live.

Jim wanted to make sure others didn't have to suffer the same way he did, so he created an idea for a foundation. At the 1993 ESPY Awards he announced the creation of the Jimmy V Foundation for Cancer Research while accepting the inaugural Arthur Ashe Courage Award. The award was created in honor of Arthur Ashe because of his work in civil rights and his participation in a delegation of 31 prominent African-Americans who visited South Africa to observe political change in the country as it approached racial integration. Jim was the first honoree for his work with students, his new foundation and his *never say never* attitude.

The most telling moment that night as he accepted the award occurred when the teleprompter told him he only had 30 seconds left to speak. He saw it, pointed and laughed, "They got that screen up there flashing 30 seconds, like I care about that screen. I got tumors all over my body, and I'm worried about some guy in the back going 30 seconds. [...] Cancer can take away all of my physical abilities. It cannot touch my mind. It cannot touch my heart and it cannot touch my soul. And those things are going to carry on forever. Don't give up. Don't ever give up." Those words remain etched into my heart and bring me to tears every time I hear them come from his lips.

I actually have a video of the speech saved on my computer and I watch it from time to time. Sadly, Jim died just eight weeks after giving that speech. But up until his death, he lived his life. And by living I mean chasing after dreams, setting up his foundation and being a father. No matter the odds, and even though Jim lost his battle, there is always a tiny chance that you will succeed and find hope from fear and victory from defeat. Even today, Jim's memory lives on through the V Foundation which has raised over $90 million dollars since 1993.[1] ESPN dedicates time every year to help raise money for the V Foundation and it's no surprise the foundation's catch-phrase is: Don't give up. Don't ever give up.

I am sure each and every one of you has stories from your life where you were defeated but rose back up again. We have all faced battles where it would have been easy to throw in the towel. The stories don't have to be as drastic as my sister's or as famous as Jim's to help you live.

THREE STAGES OF LIVING

I read a book shortly after graduating college about a mother's spiritual and emotional journey after her son committed suicide when his family refused to accept his homosexuality. Without ruining the ending, *Prayers for Bobby* ends with a story about a student who was awarded a scholarship from Bobby's family. He writes in a note to the family: "From you I can learn strength and courage. Even if it's only to survive." It is a testament not only to the struggles that confront today's youth, but of anyone trying to live.

Obviously this is an extreme case of living, but we all struggle to live our own lives. My definition of living includes going after your passions, setting goals, having dreams and living the life you want for yourself and your family. But even that scholarship winner is growing;

he is learning strength and survival in hopes that he can move through his struggles to a life that is fully lived.

Living is one of the few things that each and every one of us can do! It is absolutely possible to live! The thing I have come to realize in my life is that there will always be someone telling you that you can't do something, or you're wrong, or that your choices are bad. Of course sometimes they may be right, like anytime I try to roller-blade. But sometimes, they will flat out be wrong. Only you can make that choice.

I believe when it comes to living, there are three stages of living that people will find themselves in.

Battlers

First there are the battlers. It comes as no surprise they are currently fighting some battle. It has them struggling. They are just like that student who is just trying to survive. They may be struggling to even get out of bed, and when they do it is a strain. It could be because of a recent personal loss or a battle raging inside. Bobby was one of those people. I used to be one of those people. I used to struggle with whether or not to get out of bed in the morning and fight the battle or to just give in. It wasn't any one moment that helped me get out. Moving out of the battler stage is a slow process. In the movie, *Life as a House*, Kevin Kline's character has a line towards the end of the movie that talks about change: "You know the great thing, though, is that change can be so constant you don't even feel the difference until there is one. It can be so slow that you don't even notice that your life is better or worse, until it is. […] It happened to me."

My battle was personal, internal and external and it almost killed me. I almost gave up. If you happen to be in this stage, you're already taking a step towards pulling yourself out by reading this book – maybe even not because of anything I can say, but because you are already taking steps on your own to control your attitude. You must first understand your fight so you can start to make a plan to win the battle. Every person ends up at this stage at one time or another in life. Helping yourself get back on your feet is the key. It is possible.

For those who are struggling to feel passionate about yourself, this is for you:

Someone loves you! That's a fact. Anyone who listens to you loves you. Anyone who spends time with you, loves you. Anyone who lends a hand to you loves you. If you still don't believe me, this quote from the movie, *Love Actually*, should prove it to you: "If you look for it, I've got a sneaking suspicion ... love actually is all around."

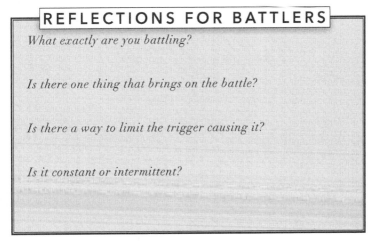

REFLECTIONS FOR BATTLERS

What exactly are you battling?

Is there one thing that brings on the battle?

Is there a way to limit the trigger causing it?

Is it constant or intermittent?

Answering these questions can help you to begin to change your internal attitude about your life and your passions and can help steer you towards finding ways to believe you have the ability to live your life.

Routine Junkies

In the middle stage of living are those people who just go through the motions. These are the people who get out of bed, go to school or work, come home, eat dinner, watch a few sit-coms and go to sleep. They may have big goals and dreams for the future but they do not act on them and so they remain in their routine. It's safe. It's comfortable. They can't get into trouble and failures are usually pretty minimal in this stage. There is absolutely nothing wrong with being in this category. Many people can make an adequate life living in this stage, if by adequate all you need is to dream but not chase it. To have passions but not share them. To have visions but not build upon them.

But I want more for you and I think you do too otherwise you probably wouldn't be reading this book. Think of Colonel Sanders. Here is a guy who had various professions throughout his life and as he neared retirement he finally took one of his dreams and started his multinational chain, *Kentucky Fried Chicken*. It began with one store. It was a nice restaurant with great patrons. Colonel Sanders perfected his recipe, now kept locked in a secret location because his one store has blossomed into 14,000 outlets in over 100 countries. He decided to stop just going through the motions and go after his dream.

Sadly, I believe the majority of people find themselves in this category more than they care to admit, but never take the leap to become the next Colonel Sanders. That's why I am writing this book – to move you to the third category. *So, are you in this stage? Do you want to move to the third?* It can be a quiet or loud process, private or public. That's what makes life great. You can go and become the next Colonel Sanders and become a thrive" or you can simply do something about your dreams and passions, not become famous and still be a "thriver." That part is up to you!

REFLECTIONS FOR ROUTINE JUNKIES

Do you stay in the routine because its easy and comfortable?

Assuming you want to change, why do you want to move into the thriver stage?

What can you change about your routine to start to thrive in life?

Thrivers

The third and final category of people is composed of those that thrive! They are the ones you see walking down the street enjoying the sunshine, stopping to smell the roses and getting wet when it rains. Of course it is more complex than that; it is really about action and attitude. Thrivers have two unique characteristics: first they not only have a dream and the passion for it, but are doing something about it. Second, thrivers often inspire others to chase their dreams. They believe that anything is possible. I have intentionally surrounded myself with people who thrive. Watching these thrivers around me pushes me to work even harder. They encourage me to take my dreams and go after them. I'm chasing after this dream right now because someone asked me a simple question: *What did you do to achieve your dreams today?* I didn't like the answer I came up with and at that moment, I became a thriver.

My paternal grandfather represents a perfect example of a quiet thriver. After his sudden passing during my mayoral campaign in 2003, we all gathered in the house where he and my grandmother had lived and raised their four children. We stayed there to make the arrangements together and entertain the people who stopped by to offer their condolences. One particular gentleman came in around lunchtime, and he quietly captivated the room with the way he spoke of my grandfather. I had never met him, but he told us a story of when he started his own business and my grandfather helped him with financial support when no one else would. It was sometime in the early 1980's and this gentleman was trying to start a recycling operation. It was very innovative for its time and no one else would support him, he said. So he asked my grandfather. My grandfather was a quiet thriver and helped him with his dream. Even my grandmother hadn't heard that story. That story was just one of many I heard that day. Total strangers recalled not just how kind and giving my grandfather was, but how he had changed their lives. While he lived a modest life in a quiet Iowa town of just 300, he lived each day by touching the lives of those around him. My grandfather is the perfect example of a thriver. He owned his own business and a small farm. On top of that, he helped and encouraged others to go after their dreams as well. When you spend your life as a thriver, you leave a legacy far beyond your years.

Reflections for Thrivers

Is there an area of your life where you are stuck in a routine and a change is needed to help you thrive even more?

What can you do today to inspire others to join you in this stage?

In February 2006, I had the good fortune of meeting Jim MacLaran at a conference in Hollywood. I had high expectations for the trip for a lot of reasons. I would be meeting dozens of new co-workers, re-connecting with a high school friend who I hadn't seen for a few years, but mostly it was a chance to hear some great speakers, meet thrivers and be inspired to become a thriver myself. The trip met all my expectations, in part because I met an exceptional man in Jim. His story has been well documented, especially since he won the Arthur Ashe Courage Award, (the same award Jim Valvano won in 1993), at the 2005 ESPYs where he received a ten-minute standing ovation. Jim, an amputee who became the fastest one-legged distance runner in the world and then became a quadriplegic in a second horrific accident, has dedicated his life to changing the world. After his accidents, Jim's friends wanted to support his recovery. From their efforts grew the Challenged Athletes Foundation. The website of the Challenged Athletes Foundation describes the birth of this foundation:[2]

> CAF grew out of a desire to assist one athlete – trailblazing below-knee-amputee endurance racer Jim MacLaren – who suffered a

devastating second accident while competing in a triathlon. Hit by a car during the bike leg, Jim was paralyzed from the neck down. His many friends quickly decided to raise funds for his recovery, and organized the first San Diego Triathlon Challenge (SDTC) – an annual fundraising triathlon event at La Jolla Cove. From this modest beginning arose a more important mission – to make sure that people with physical challenges have the same freedom to enjoy sports that the rest of us take for granted.

Through his two accidents, Jim still works with his foundation and is changing the lives of children and adults all around the world. I cannot even begin to express how impressed I am with how Jim conducts his life. It wasn't all rosy after his accidents and he admittedly found himself in the group of battlers. But he fought through and decided he had to live. There were no other options. He had to thrive to help himself and to help others. When you thrive, you help others and at the same time, almost magically, your drive to thrive grows.

So what keeps you from thriving? Imagine if we had a world full of thrivers. I think there are more of us out there, but for some reason there are those who stay in the routine junkies stage. My biggest challenge, my life's mission, is to change lives. I aim to change the lives of the people I meet, by helping them examine themselves in the hopes that they will come to believe that it is in their capacity to thrive – to live. I believe this mission to be at the very core of my being.

I believe the most crucial factor in whether or not you thrive, the single largest barrier to that outcome, is simply how you feel about yourself. It's 100 percent attitude. The bad news is that this means it is entirely up to you, no one else can change this for you. But the amazing news is that it's absolutely up to you – and that means it is entirely within your grasp! I know it because I've been there. I have been in the battle. I have been a routine junkie. I had a pour attitude when it came to my dreams and goals and the life I wanted. But I also know because I'm not there anymore.

If you're not passionate about yourself and your dreams, it is exponentially harder to *live* your life. This chapter is focused on you! It is about you – living. It is about you grabbing your life by the horns and steering yourself to where you want to go. You are in control. No one else is in control but you.

Never give up on life. Challenges and failures will always exist. I have already had my fair share of them and I'm sure you have as well. I can't promise more won't come along, but I can promise your that no matter what, it *will* be worth it. The great thing about life is that we get to live it! You get to live it according to your choices and your attitude. Never forget that you have that power!

Join the chase. Join the fight. Jump on the train of your life! The fun part is that you get to choose to live and thrive!

The creation of a thousand forests is in one acorn. Go now, take root, and live!

Points to Remember

» Living is a choice: "The creation of a thousand forests is in one acorn." Take root in your life!

» Struggles in life often give you opportunities to live again.

» Battlers are struggling to live. Just focus on changing one thing today, one thing tomorrow, until you are living again.

» If you're in a routine, find a way to break out of it by taking a risk to start living your dream.

» Meet thrivers every chance you have and add them to your support time

» Never give up on your life and living your passions.

Chapter 5

Try Anything and Everything

"ANYONE WHO HAS NEVER MADE A MISTAKE
HAS NEVER TRIED ANYTHING NEW."

-Albert Einstein

Your challenge should you choose to accept it is to make your life one big great adventure. My meaning here is simple, but it is hard to express in one sentence. Friends and mentors have said a certain phrase to me while I'm stressing over a big decision like taking a job with a political campaign or starting my own company. What everyone always tells me is that "life is a journey." They say I shouldn't worry about the outcome so much and just enjoy the experience of the present moment and the possibilities of the future. In this life, you get to create your own journey. Grammy award-winning artist and one of the top 100 best selling musicians of all time, Gloria Estefan, tells us what to do: "[…] life is a journey, and every step of the way, we can learn something and become stronger and wiser."

At some point in my junior year of high school, I decided it could be fun to try out the speech team. I was good at giving speeches in class and I thought maybe competing would be fun. It must also be noted that my teacher at the time was also the speech coach and has helped me edit this book as well. Event after I joined the team I was scared of my ability to win and do well. But in the choice I made the decision to enjoy the journey I had chosen to embark upon. What I found out from my first competition was that I was pretty good. Through many before school and after school practice sessions, I perfected my speech for that spring's district competition and to my surprise, I scored a Division I rating and moved onto the next round. Again, I scored Division I and I earned an All-State award and an invitation to give my speech at the All-State event. The award now sits on my bookshelf next to my desk to remind me to take risks and try new things as often as I can. Because of that experience, I'm writing this book. No one asked me to join the team; I chose the path and took the challenge deciding to enjoy the journey instead of being afraid of the destination.

You get to choose your chapter titles and the adventures your character gets to go on. "Living Life at Performance Level™" is the name of a keynote speech by speaker and performer Curtis Zimmerman. He speaks about how we are the leading actors in the drama that is our lives. A common question asked in ice-breaker activities revolves around who would play you in a Hollywood movie. You shouldn't hesitate to cast yourself in your own life! *Who better to play your life and your passions than you?* Better yet, you've already been cast so you have to live it and experience it.

In Josh Kilmer-Purcell's first fiction book, *Candy Everybody Wants,* he tackles the idea of being the leading actor in your life. The main character, Jayson, wants fame and fortune and a life in Hollywood, including all the lights, flashbulbs, elegant parties, and the Oscars of course. Through the antics of his teenage friends and his runaway adventure to New York, Jayson learns that sometimes having everything you want isn't always the best thing. He realizes that you can't change your script, but you can change your reaction to it. Sometimes in our quest for happiness, we forget to enjoy the journey. We forget that it is the experience and how we respond to each event along the way that matters the most.

This chapter is about casting you in the role of you! The catch is that not only will you be the lead in your show, you're also the director, the executive producer, the financier, the protagonist and the antagonist, the victor and the villain. Some of the casting is up to you. Parents, teachers and siblings are cast by the network, so we just have to live with them. You have a choice with the rest of your supporting cast. What you can control is how you live your life. You can choose to pick up the basketball even if you are in a wheelchair. You can choose to join a club that is foreign to your way of thinking in the hopes of learning something new. You can decide to get up an hour earlier everyday to read more or write more or get in some exercise in the morning before work or school.

The last chapter focused on living. That's what we are on Earth to do. In order to live in the best and most fulfilling way possible, you must be willing to try anything and everything. This chapter will be broken up into two sections. First, you must look at your life experiences and what you want to try. Then you need to look at challenges or obstacles in your life that get in your way. Let's get started!

BE WILLING TO CHANGE THE SCRIPT

According to Kramer, a character on *Seinfeld*, if there is a proctologist at a party, sit right next to them because you'll hear great stories all night long. "It was a million to one, doc. A million to one." Do you ever wonder why the most popular people at parties are the most popular? I believe there are two possible reasons. Either they are great story tellers, or they simply have a lot of stories to tell. Usually it is almost always a mix of the two. That's what your life is. Life is a million experiences that you will have the opportunity to either grasp or let slip through your fingers.

Until I was 24, I wouldn't have anything to do with straight brewed coffee. I would only have "foo-foo" drinks like lattes and mochas. I even fought drinking tea for the longest time. The reason for disliking both was simple: I had a bad first experience. Then one day I decided to give them both another try. I ordered a coffee and with fear for my tongue and trepidation that I just wasted $2 on a cup of terribly flavored water that I may not like, I tipped back the cup. To my surprise, it wasn't bad. So I gave coffee another chance the next time I went to the coffee shop. Now, more times than not, I'll order a coffee. I afforded myself the opportunity to enjoy something I had never enjoyed before. I'm thankful

I recast coffee and tea back into my life.

When I was seven, I had a bad first experience with cherries. My family was out having dinner at a local buffet in town that my uncle managed and somehow a cherry ended up on my plate. I ate it. Of course, looking back on it, the cherry was probably fine, but it was the first time my seven-year-old mouth tasted a cherry and I didn't like it! The texture was all wrong and it didn't taste like my cherry Kool-Aid at all. I spit it out back onto my plate. From then on, for 15 years, I wouldn't have anything to do with cherries. No cherry toppings. No cherry pie. I did enjoy cherry flavored suckers, but that's only because I knew the value of high fructose corn syrup.

Then one day my friend Eric put Jell-O with cherries in it on my plate. Eric always made interesting meals when I visited. We recently had a good laugh as we reminisced over the meals he'd make when I would visit. He recalled one time he wanted to make chocolate chip pancakes. But without chocolate chips, he used a broken up candy bar instead. We both laughed thinking about how bad they turned out. We did both still each the pancakes. With him looking on I was faced with a choice: refuse my friends' dessert or recast my own role in my life. I took the high road, shaky and with visions of my first cherry encounter dancing in my head. I put the cherries in my mouth and the texture was new, weird and my mouth had no idea what to think. Yeah ... I loved it! My life has been changed ever since. Maybe not in a big way – let's be honest, I just add cherries to the shopping list every once in a while, but I also found that I could eat new desserts and enjoy a whole new fruit-imbued list of foods. But it was, in a way, a huge, yet small step that I still think about. Even more, I am glad I took that chance!

Or even more difficult maybe, *what bad experiences have you let become an excuse to not doing something you know could be good for you?* Maybe it is time to directly challenge everything in your script. For instance, if you quit trying to learn how to ride a bike after the first fall, you'd still be walking to work. (Though I am assuming here that your methods of transportation wouldn't have progressed any further, so maybe it's a stretch to say you wouldn't be driving now. But go along with me here.) If you stopped eating vegetables since your mom made you as a kid, maybe it's time to pick the fork back up! It may not be fun, but it is definitely healthy for your body and mind to eat that spinach. I can attest to eating spinach and asparagus which I started eating in earnest for the first time in the last year. Take those bad experiences and don't just blast past them, instead let them open (maybe just small) doors to new experiences. Trust me. It's time!

For me, these experiences of going outside my comfort zone demonstrate how important it is to be willing to try something new, even if you've had a bad first experience.

REFLECTIONS

How will going outside your comfort zone be reflected in your life?

What bad experiences have you had that you would like to give a second chance?

In the book *Presentation Zen* by Garr Reynolds, the author writes that children are free to do as they please. They will sit and color, paint, imaginate with Play-Doh for hours and not self-judge or self-sensor, simply because they are kids and haven't formulated any idea of stunting their own creativity. Adults on the other hand tell themselves they aren't creative, that they can't paint or draw. My boyfriend finished his degree in Fashion Design last summer, and he's told me that there have been countless times that he hears people tell him how much they wish there were creative like him, but that they just can't draw. They don't even say it's hard, or that they aren't the best at it. They say they can't. When this is happened, the antagonist has taken over the script of your life. The lights are down low and the music is mysterious. He is constantly shocked at not just how many say it, but that almost always it is people who haven't actually tried since childhood. Sometimes he laughs, because he knows it doesn't matter! If you want to create, draw, paint or design, go do it! Don't say you can't. If quality and technical skills are a concern, then go learn! That's the amazing thing – people who say *can't* often *don't*. They remain case as the antagonist instead of changing the script. Take a night class – take ten classes! I actually used to be one of those people that said I couldn't create. I would see my boyfriend paint and every time I would think, wow those are awesome! I wish I could paint like that!" He would laugh and then tell me to just go do it.

Six months after I met him I bought my first tubes of paint and some brushes. Two years after that, I have shown my work in a local art show and in a local coffee shop. I have no idea how good I am, but that's not the point. I did it … I painted! As a human being you have been given the gift of unlimited possibility, and that includes your mind and your ability to experience anything and everything. One thing you should never do is say "can't" unless a doctor says so or you've tried and completely proven that it just won't work. And I know there are things in your life right now that need to be recast. Magic-Eye books? I have never been able to see one of the illusions, but you can bet every time I see a book, I pick it up and take a quick peak. I'm going to keep trying until I see something!

During a presentation at the Beyond Rubies Conference at Kirkwood Community College in March of 2008, I put up an image of a Birds of Paradise flower at the end of my presentation. A woman in the front row interrupted me and said, "You should paint that!" At the time I laughed her off. I thought, "Yeah right. I can't paint that."

Almost immediately though, I started to think about what she said. The challenge wouldn't leave my mind. Both my internal reaction and my external response ate at me. I was angry at myself for saying I couldn't do it. Looking back on it I realize that my reaction was probably pretty typical of most of us when faced with such a daunting idea, but that really isn't an excuse at all. Hours after the presentation ended, I was still kicking myself for my reaction. It hit me on my drive back home like a ton a bricks and I vowed that not only would I not say that again, but I also vowed to do something about it. That one negative response has turned into an incredible motivation to surpass my own expectations. I finally attempted the painting in October of 2008. I wanted it to be perfect. I wanted to show myself that I could do it. I wanted to show the audience that I could do it. With the photo in front of me, I spent hours focusing on the colors and how to make them blend and mix the right way to make it realistic. To this day, it remains the best painting I've done. This is true because I felt challenged by my inner demons not only by the task of the painting itself but also by my own attitude which was the true inspiration for this piece of art. This success was as much about the outcome as it was the journey. I decided to rewrite part of my script to not stop myself, instead choosing to live and experience my life.

REFLECTIONS

What are you afraid of trying?

What do you think is unattainable in your life?

Do you think this because of someone else's comments or actions?

What steps can you take today to change the way you react to negative inner thoughts?

When talking about thinking we cannot achieve something, Henry Ford said it best, "Whether you think you can or whether you think you can't, you're right." While in college at the University of Northern Iowa my neighbors in the dorm, Jarred and Jeff, worked out a few times a week at our recreation center. I always refused to go with them. I didn't want to work out. I wasn't a "muscle-head" or a jock and I knew

I wasn't very muscular or strong and thus I hated to lift weights with other people who could actually, well, lift weights. Plus, I didn't think I was built to work out. My body was just skin and bones and I had tried to get into working out during high school, but I never saw any results. In high school, I didn't enjoy doing it because my of my friends didn't work out. Plus I didn't want to put in the work of doing it multiple times per week. But now I suddenly had friends who worked out and wanted me to join them. Shortly after Christmas break I started joining them. I'm not sure what finally made me decide to join, but maybe it was a result of their constant asking me to go.

I remember my first trip to the gym with them. It was January and the cold air was biting through my sweatpants. Why on Earth these guys did this multiple times a week eluded me. The first time was rough, but Jarred and Jeff encouraged me the whole time because they knew I was uncomfortable being there and quietly second guessing my own abilities and coming up with an excuse not to come the next time. After the first day at the gym, I saw the potential. Not a huge body, but a healthy body. Soon, I was knocking on their doors, urging them to go work out with me.

One time in particular we were doing the bench press and out of the three of us, I always benched the lowest weight. On this night it was just the bar and some small additional weights for me, but I kept pushing myself to not necessarily lift more than my friends, but to reach my personal goals. On my second set in the rotation that night, I was set to bench around 170 pounds, the most weight I had tried up to that point. I got myself comfortable on the bench with my feet squarely on the ground. My hands were chalked up and my mind was focused for this battle. I looked up at Jeff who was there to spot me and he said, "You can do it Rich." I put my hands into position, focused on my mission and pushed up. I now had all the weight on my arms and my meager chest. I brought the bar down and pushed back quickly to get the bar back to the top, but I struggled. Jeff, noticing my inability to push the bar back to the top, helped me get the bar back up. I immediately jumped off the bench and stormed out of the gym. I was really upset.

I had been working for two months to get stronger and after all the time and work I couldn't even bench my own body weight. I felt like an absolute failure. I sat down outside the weight room and thought about what had just happened and why I got to that point where I gave up. My attitude has always been to not quit. Two minutes after walking out, I walked back in to prove to myself I could do it. And I did! I wasn't going to let myself stop me. Since I'm the producer and the star of my life, I get to decide when I succeed and when I fail. If the weight ended up being too much, then I was willing to live with that. But I wasn't going to let my mind beat me. My mind had been telling me for years that I wasn't made to be a guy that went to the gym.

That's what experiencing life is all about. When it comes to living your life, you have to let it be experienced … by you! The more and more you do that, the more you will find those previously scary or impossible experiences not so bad, or even amazing. Better yet, in the process you are likely to find new ones you enjoy, and ones that you never before could have even predicted. Sharing these experiences with others in your performance can help empower the people around you to do the same.

I know I am always watching my friends and colleagues to see their latest adventures. Sometimes I ask to join them on their journeys and other times I take from their experiences and create my own. When you live your life for the experiences, you allow your life to be plot driven, full of rising and falling action as opposed to the never ending story where the bad guy always wins.

CAST YOURSELF AS THE VICTOR

Now that we have talked about trying new experiences, let's take a look at some of the obstacles that may be getting in our way. Obstacles come from many sources, whether it is a boss, a company, a spouse, or just the world at large. The key thing to remember is that obstacles do not have to be seen as undefeatable. Make no mistake; I know these obstacles are very real and very hard to overcome. I also know one thing for certain: you will never overcome your obstacles if you don't challenge them. The reward is so often much greater than the risk and sometimes in part because you took that risk, the reward will be so much sweeter.

My friend Asitha who I introduced in Chapter 2, represents perfectly the idea of taking on a challenge and succeeding. It was Christmas 2004 and the news came in the early morning hours of December 26, but because I attended a family event all day, I didn't hear about the devastating Asian tsunami until I returned home. It wiped out portions of his native Sri Lanka. Asitha called me soon after I saw the news that evening, heartbroken and said he wanted to do something. We both didn't know what, but we knew we were going to do something to help. Over the next two weeks and over many discussions, I helped him formulate a plan to help rebuild his country. We bounced a number of ideas and I could tell by his passion that he was going to try everything he could to make a difference.

He organized a fundraiser where he sold white-silicone wristbands with, "12-26-2004 HOPE" embossed on them. Over the course of about a month, Asitha, his family and his friends raised over $5,000 in our small community to help rebuild Sri Lanka. The local newspaper even wrote a story about their effort. That money went to build two new houses in Sri Lanka. Asitha just wanted to make a difference and wasn't sure how, but he was willing to try anything to help. The challenge for Asitha was not only coming up with an idea to raise the money, but also the execute it and make it happen. A world away from the devastation, he raised awareness in the community and it ended with people calling him to find ways to support the cause.

Too many times when we have a challenge in front of us, we put up a wall and think that the barrier cannot possibly be overcome. This is a bad habit to get into because not only do you use the word "not" which are you using the word "not," which by now we have learned to eliminate, but you also don't even try. You have heard the cliché: If at first you don't succeed, try, try again.

Many of the external obstacles or challenges in your life may seem like they are insurmountable. From a bad manager, a failing company, an emotional spouse or just the world, each challenge must be measured to determine if it can be overcome. For instance, in a bad economy, sometimes living with the bad manager is the only way to go, but if you're up to it and you have a great idea, start your own company! I started my company not because of any external factor, but because I knew I wanted to be my own boss and control my own dream.

Over the last year, I have joined forces with Kiva, a micro-lending organization that supports entrepreneurs around the world. For awhile I've wanted to support missions to the Third-World but not through the traditional channels. Kiva's concept is quite simple. I make a loan to an entrepreneur in another country and the entrepreneur pays it back over the determined loan period. I get the money back and I loan it back out to someone new. To date I have loaned over $500 spread out over fifteen business owners. It's a small thing, but I know it's helping people in need. Making change isn't always easy but working to overcome the obstacles in these parts world can lead to some amazing outcomes. The same goes for your life. It is not easy to break down your barriers, but the opportunities that may arise from trying everything and anything to reach your dream can lead to untold success.

REFLECTIONS

What barrier do you currently refuse to attack?

What causes you to let this wall remain?

If you wanted to, what could you do to begin to tear down that barrier?

One external barrier keeping me from trying something I want to do is my body. It isn't made for long-distance running. All my life, I've never been good at running, much less a fan of it. First of all, the only sport I played in high school was tennis. Unlike track and cross country, tennis only requires short bursts of running, thus I'd never worked to run for longer than a minute or two. But after getting into the habit of going to the gym, I have found that I enjoy the time I spend on the road or path, just running. A goal I've toiled with actually chasing after is running a marathon. That would be 26.2 miles of non-stop knee-jarring, lung-gasping, pavement-pounding endurance for a person who gets pretty tired after four miles on the treadmill. So, I have made it a goal. In fact, I recently added it to my *Life To Do List*, and I will achieve it. I plan on attacking this goal but in order to so effectively, like any good producer, I must make a plan. I need to understand what a marathon will do to my body and how to train for it the best way possible. When you decide to tackle something, you have to be realistic about where you are now, and what it will take to get there. It may be more than you're willing to handle at once, but like saving for your first bike, taking it one step at a time pays off.

When I started running in earnest a year ago, running two miles was enough for my lungs and my legs. A year later, I've more than doubled that. It's not a huge accomplishment, but I'm proud of it and plan on going longer as I keep training. Asitha and I recently made a deal that we would both run our first marathon within a year of his finishing medical school. Having someone around you to help you through the tough moments when you want to quit, or just maybe don't want to put on the shoes for the six-mile fun run will help you overcome the low-points that come from any challenge. This goal will be an immense challenge to achieve, but with Asitha there with me, providing the support and motivation, I have no doubt I'll enter and do everything in my power to complete the marathon.

I put *running a marathon* on my *Life To Do List* because I feel that it is important to write those things down. If it's not out of site, it's harder to be out of mind! Not only is it important to write down your short term and long term goals and formulate a plan on how to achieve them, but it's also important to write down those things that you want to experience at some point in your life. *This is your script, remember?* You get to decide the plot twists and turns and when you will take a random trip to Italy or splurge and take a painting class.

Do you have a "to do" list for your life? This list isn't that you want to have a certain amount of money in the bank, but you could say that you want to have a retirement home in France. These are more experienced-based and things you want to be able to tell stories about. These aren't meant to have a deadline, just so long as they are completed in your lifetime. Just to give you an idea, below is my *Life To Do List* (current as of 31 December 2009) .

Richard's Life To Do List
1. Set foot in all four oceans
   a. Atlantic (Completed July 2004)
   b. Pacific (Completed May 2006)
   c. Indian
   d. Arctic
2. Visit all seven continents
   a. Asia
   b. Africa
   c. Antarctica
   d. Australia
   e. North America
   f. South America
   g. Europe
3. Touch a pyramid in Egypt
4. Eat chocolates in Germany
5. Have a picnic under the Eiffel Tower
6. Take the picture with the Leaning Tower of Pisa
7. See the Mona Lisa
8. Fly first class
9. Lay on the beach in Sri Lanka
10. Attend a Presidential Inauguration
11. Drink wine in a vineyard in Italy
12. Attending the following events
    a. Wimbledon
    b. US Open (tennis) (Completed September 2007)
    c. US Open (golf)
    d. The Masters
    e. The Super Bowl
    f. Australian Open
    g. French Open

    h.   A White Tie event

    i.   And evening gala fundraiser

13. Attend a show on Broadway

14. Attend a show at the Kodak Theatre

15. Sell a painting

16. Touch the Berlin Wall

17. Visit (actual locations):

    a.   Gettysburg Battlefield

    b.   D-Day Battlefield

    c.   Auschwitz

    d.   Cape Canaveral

    e.   President Reagan Library

    f.   World Trade Center

    g.   Oklahoma City Memorial (Completed August 2008)

    h.   Independence Hall

    i.   Fenway Park

    j.   Monk's Restaurant (from Seinfeld)

    k.   Soup Nazi Restaurant (from Seinfeld)

18. Visit (Countries):

    a.   Sri Lanka

    b.   Iraq

    c.   South Africa

    d.   Russia

    e.   England

    f.   France

    g.   Spain

    h.   Portugal

    i.   Slovakia

    j.   Lithuania

    k.   Canada

    l.   Alaska

    m.   Bosnia

19. Write a full-length novel (Completed July 2008)

20. Publish a book (Completed February 2010)

21. Publish a novel

22. Have a book signing

23. Produce a clothing line

24. Backpack through the Rocky Mountains

25. Backpack through New Zealand

26. Have Baklava in Greece

27. Have Vegemite in Australia

28. Run in Central Park

29. Skydive
30. Ice Skate in Rockefeller Plaza
31. Host a formal dinner party
32. Give a keynote address (Rockhurst University on April 27, 2008)
33. Play in the National Olympics
34. Play Asitha in tennis
35. Have a picture drawn of me while in Europe
36. Walk the streets of Paris
37. Deliver a eulogy
38. Own a house
39. Have my parents attend my wedding
40. See the Stanley Cup
41. Camp outside
42. Start my own company (Completed June 2007)
43. Paint a self-portrait
44. Ride RAGBRI
45. Give commencement speech (Completed May 2002)
46. Run a half-marathon
47. Run a full marathon
48. Own a farm
49. Get a hole-in-one in golf
50. Play a links golf course (preferably in Scotland)
51. See the Sistine Chapel
52. Visit St. Peter's Basilica
53. See the David (Galleria dell'Accademia, Florence)

The obvious obstacle I have faced in writing this book is actually writing it. But here I am on a Saturday morning, sitting in my local coffee shop, pounding away at the keyboard. A month before I started to write, I looked at the calendar and blocked out the time I was going to need to write the first draft. I put it on the calendar. Most importantly, I didn't let anything get in the way. I wrote every day I said I would. One of my biggest barriers to success in life is my ability and willingness to push my own objectives to the back-burner. With this book I have been successful in overcoming that and I'm better for it. I had that level of focus because I believe so much in the potential of this book to change your life.

You must be willing to change the script of your life and then cast yourself as the victor. All the things you have told yourself you weren't good at or didn't like, challenge all those beliefs. Once you do that, see yourself being successful. Again, you are the director of your life and this show will turn out however you want it to. Starting a *Life To Do List* can offer you help on the journey. You have to be willing to try anything and everything to write the script you want and live the dream you have. If you do that, the Oscar will be a lock. Like Gloria Estefan said about life, "[…] every step of the way, we can learn something and become stronger and wiser." All my experiences have made me a much stronger and wiser person. My million experiences have prepared me for this book.

Points to Remember

- » You get to choose your chapter titles and the adventures your character gets to go on.

- » "Anyone who has never made a mistake has never tried anything new." -Albert Einstein

- » Cast yourself as the victor in your life.

- » If you want to create, draw, paint or design, go do it! Don't ever say you can't do something until you've failed as much as you possibly can.

- » When it comes to living your life, you have to let it be experienced by you.

- » Be willing to change the script.

- » Create a Life To Do List.

Dare to…

Now that you have analyzed your thoughts by picking apart bad habits and looking into the reasons you do the things you do, it's time to start challenging yourself. It is time to push yourself to achieve great new heights. It is time to take another step. It is time to start taking actions!

Every day that you challenge yourself to be a better person and put yourself in the right frame of mind to believe in your full potential, anything is possible!

"YOU ARE THE WAY YOU ARE BECAUSE
THAT'S THE WAY YOU WANT TO BE.
IF YOU REALLY WANTED TO BE ANY
DIFFERENT, YOU WOULD BE IN THE
PROCESS OF CHANGING RIGHT NOW."

-Fred Smith

Chapter 6

Overcome

"A JOURNEY OF A THOUSAND MILES MUST
BEGIN WITH A SINGLE STEP."

-Confucius

It is finally time to focus on things I believe you need to *do*, actions you must make a part of your daily life to begin chasing your dreams. The list of people who have overcome great obstacles is long. Off the top of my head, that list includes Dennis Bryd, Jim MacLaren, Richard Collier, Charles Dickens, Wayman Tisdale, John Amechi and my sister … those are just a few people who have overcome great obstacles. Of course those are some pretty famous people, but there are millions of people that you have never heard of that have done just as great things. Think about the people in your life right now who it could be. Someone who comes to my mind is my friend Asitha who I have written about in previous chapters. He's overcome the red tape of the United Nations and also helped rebuild homes after the tsunami of 2004. He continues to inspire me every day. We all have amazing examples around us of people that can inspire us and also serve as the motivating factor as you move to tackle the obstacle that looms in front of you. Sometimes the obstacles in your life are those huge Sunday night, made-for-TV movie epics like overcoming a terrible disease or catching the tiger that escaped from the zoo. Others are those small battles, like having a stressful day but still nailing the presentation, having a fight with your spouse only to still be a wonderful parent and read a book to your kids at bedtime. Each of these obstacles includes that little voice on your shoulder that you simply need to quiet in order to listen to the other voice; the voice of possibility, of change, of belief in yourself to achieve great things.

There are two things you need to think about when striving to overcome the obstacles, big or small, in your life. First, analyze whether or not the obstacle is small and could be solved in five minutes or if it is one of those life-changing situations that might suck the life out of you to tackle. Second, ask yourself who around you has either gone through something similar or who you can ask for help.

If it is a small obstacle, take care of it and move on. Simple as that. If it is one of the bigger challenges, then take the time. Plan out how you will battle it. Think about the things you will going to need to sustain yourself and the pros and cons of fighting the battle. That leads to the importance of the second question about finding out if anyone around you has fought a similar battle. Too often we spin our wheels too much when people around us may have fought a similar battle and could share their expertise.

BE THE AUTHENTIC YOU

In my opinion, the greatest president the United States has ever seen was Abraham Lincoln. I firmly believe that without his leadership, steadfastness, belief in others and his never failing kindness, the Civil War would have permanently divided the country in two. Not only did he have to overcome his own shortcomings, such as living far from the Washington power circle in Illinois and being regarded as a "woodsman" and not a smart leader. He had also only won one election prior to the Presidential Election of 1860. But once nominated on the Republican ticket, he took to the task of building a coalition that would not only support the preservation of the Union, but also bring opposing viewpoints to the table. One of the foremost biographies on Lincoln, written by noted historian Doris Kearns Goodwin, says it all in the title: *Team of Rivals*. In order to build his coalition, he put his best supporters and also some of the most ardent rivals in his Cabinet. Doing so allowed him to put the voices of dissention inside his office and allowed to show a unified front to the country.

During his entire administration, he routinely accepted the blame for the missteps of his Generals and Cabinet members; even if he wasn't directly responsible. Two of his four sons didn't make it to adulthood. On top of it all, he only had the support of – at best – half the country. Talk about odds stacked against you!

Through it all, Lincoln overcame the odds, preserved the Union and overcame every political obstacle in his path for one simple reason: he believed in his heart it was in the country's best interest to remain together and that fundamentally, slavery was wrong. There were definitely bumps along the way and he had to relieve commanders of command and maneuver efforts to undermine his Cabinet, but Lincoln never lost sight of the purpose his Presidency had taken.

I took a trip to Washington D.C. in the fall of 2006 and my list of places to go included Ford's Theatre and the Petersen House. The theatre is where Lincoln was shot and the Petersen House just across the street is where he was taken after the shooting and subsequently died hours later. They are pieces of American history and I wanted to experience them first-hand. At the time of his assassination, Lincoln had just been re-elected to the Presidency and had finally achieved his goal of preserving the Union. As I walked down the street, it didn't seem possible that Lincoln had walked on this very narrow coble-stone road. I found it emotionally challenging to stand outside President Lincoln's theatre box, just feet away from where he was shot. Knowing that Lincoln's last moments were in the booth right before me, but also knowing that one of the Nation's greatest presidents had been killed right where I was standing took my breath away. It was the one thing Lincoln could not overcome, but through his leadership and belief in his own strengths and abilities, he helped save the country and is a true representation of someone who has overcome the odds.

It could be argued that Lincoln's success was due to his level of involvement in the execution of the war, his Cabinet and his ability to work and communicate with all different types of people. But there is more to it than that. As I said, with only half the country supporting the cause of the Union, he had to overcome continual political threats to his leadership and threats from those who were on the fence about the war itself. He had to overcome his family's own mortality. He had to overcome politicians who were losing their faith in him.

How does President Lincoln apply to you? It's quite simple really. When it comes to your life and your dreams and passions, you have to do whatever it takes to make your life yours. If you believe you have to go back to school because you hate your job and your true passion is teaching, then go be a teacher! Rarely will any of us be faced with the life and death choices Lincoln had to make, but perhaps we will. Perhaps overcoming your personal challenges is your battlefield. Maybe it is your friends saying you should spend your time doing something and shouldn't take a certain risk. I believe being true to yourself and your convictions is your life and death choice. In the end, that becomes the true measure of a life, the level of truth in how you lived your life. Lincoln stacked his presidency on the preservation of the Union and ultimately the eradication of slavery, *what will you be staking your life on?*

It's still hard to forget the tumultuous times of the 2000 presidential campaign when Senator John McCain and Governor George W. Bush were in a neck-and-neck battle for the Republican nomination for president. After falling behind in the early polls, McCain went back to the basics and developed a new strategy, focusing his energies on the "Straight Talk Express." He traveled the country telling Americans like it was and refusing to sugar-coat America's problems. This factor alone is what endeared him to so many supporters despite his well-publicized temper and other special quirks. Much to the electorate's surprise, McCain won the New Hampshire primary and thus the candidates went on to Super Tuesday. The winner that day would be the de-facto nominee. As the race became more competitive, Bush went to his base and the Evangelicals, and with that message and group he secured the nomination and sent McCain back to the Senate. But McCain didn't stop.

He created a Political Action Committee, "Straight Talk America", and for the next eight years worked for all Americans through this group. He traveled the country continuing to tell it like it was. I had the great opportunity to meet Senator McCain in 2006 in his build-up for the presidential campaign of 2008. While visiting my hometown of Mason City, Iowa, on a stop to drum up support for a local candidate; he stopped at a fundraiser to give a rousing speech and meet with potential future staffers of a presidential campaign team. Everyone there that night knew he was starting his presidential campaign. At the close of the event he took questions from attendees, and I took the opportunity of getting in a question.

I was sitting in the front of the room and I asked very simply, "Why hasn't Congress done something about Social Security?" What I saw that evening was a man who wasn't afraid of politics or his career, but a man who should be in the Oval Office. He looked around the room then back at me and said so a matter-of-factly, it took me by surprise: "Because we're scared." In that moment I fell in love with the Senator and all he stood for. A year later his campaign fell apart. But just like he did in 2000, he retooled and got back on message. He staged a huge comeback to overtake every Republican contender to win the nomination. He, of course, went on to lose the general election to Barack Obama, but in the end he was vintage McCain:

"I am so deeply grateful to all of you for the great honor of your support and for all you have done for me. I wish the outcome had been different, my friends. The road was a difficult one from the outset. But your support and friendship never wavered. I cannot adequately express how deeply indebted I am to you. […] A lost election will never mean more to me than the privilege of your faith and friendship. […] This campaign was and will remain the great honor of my life. […] Today, I was a candidate for the highest office in the country I love so much. And tonight, I remain Her servant. That is blessing enough for anyone and I thank the people of Arizona for it."

Back in 2000 and then again in 2008, McCain had to overcome the establishment conservatives to get his message out and each time, even though he didn't win the final election, he was successful. He overcame the odds again in 2008 when all the pundits said he was too old, didn't have the money and didn't have the votes to win the nomination. For eight years and for his whole career he has remained true to himself, earning a place in America's hearts. It also allowed him to say what he said the night of the 2008 general election, that the campaign was the honor of his life.

While both of these men, Lincoln and McCain are internationally known and respected, they are still people just like you and me. They had challenges to overcome, both large and small. Both of them made choices to give them opportunities to be strong and advance their own lives, overcoming their obstacles in the process. They both knew their strengths and weaknesses and used their talents to further their careers.

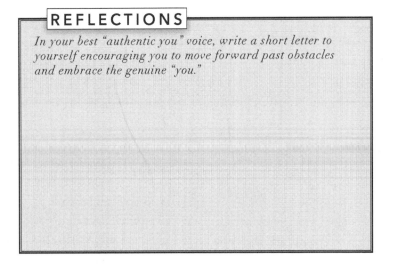

REFLECTIONS

In your best "authentic you" voice, write a short letter to yourself encouraging you to move forward past obstacles and embrace the genuine "you."

FAILURE IS NOT AN OPTION

In the fall of 2008, I was writing biographies for new inductees to a local hall of fame. At the time, I was working for the United States Tennis Association and this woman was being inducted into their Hall of Fame. I knew from her nomination and the voting process that she was seriously ill. She sounded energetic as I began to interview her over the phone her about tennis and volunteer background, but I could hear in her voice that she was tired. I felt optimistic that this woman I had never met was fighting hard and would make it through. We talked for about twenty minutes and I could tell she had enjoyed her time spent with tennis. She told me she started playing because her husband had played. I asked her about her fight with cancer. It was wearing her out and she was honest with me that it was a tough fight. As I neared the end of the interview, I had one more question to ask and what she said in response has stuck with me. She said, "I will play tennis again." At the induction ceremony, her friend gave her acceptance speech, as she was too weak to attend herself. Just 24 hours later, she passed away. Even though I never met this woman in person, I was saddened because in her heart I know she planned on getting back to living her life cancer-free. She had fervor for life and I'm glad I had the opportunity to have a twenty-minute conversation with her. Here is my point: although she didn't overcome her cancer, she didn't let the cancer overtake her. She controlled her emotions, thoughts and attitude as shown in her *I will play tennis again* comment.

According to the American Cancer Society, there were nearly 1.5 million people afflicted with cancer in 2008.[1] Coupled with that, it is said that at some point in your life you'll either have cancer yourself or someone you know will be affected by it. Still in my 20s, I am already a part of that statistic. In fact, the first time I came to know cancer was when Janet* *(name changed)*, a family friend of ours Jane* (name changed) returned from a trip and found that she had cancer. I have since had a few family members become afflicted with the disease. The people in my life battled cancer successfully and it is a constant reminder of the power of positive thought. I know not many other words can strike as much fear or sorrow in someone's life like cancer can.

Back in the early days of HIV and AIDS, it was killing every person who contracted the deadly virus and, while according to the World Health Organization[2] it still plagues 33 million people around the globe today, it is slowly becoming one of those things you can live with. It isn't any less deadly and it certainly isn't a cake-walk. The "cocktail" is the most successful treatment on the market[3] but it comes at an enormous financial cost, as well as the impact it has on each and every day. Living with it should probably be changed to *living in spite of it*, but that is just the point. The people living with any affliction have shown it is possible to overcome it and live a pretty normal life. It doesn't mean totally getting rid of a disease; the overcoming part of the victory comes from allowing yourself to live your life as normally and passionately as possible. No matter what is going on in your life, around you, to you, or in you, don't let it overtake you. You may never be able to defeat something, but that doesn't mean you can't win. A failure happens only when you decide to give up.

REFLECTIONS

What is something you would like to overcome today?

What is something you'd like to overcome in ten years?

Becoming afflicted with deceases like cancer and HIV will undoubtedly change your life. They are big obstacles to overcome. It is important to keep a positive attitude when faced with similar challenges, but also have an attitude with everything in your life that failure is not an option. If you couldn't think of something you'd like to challenge and overcome, you need to dig deeper. It may be hard to think of something big, but the size of the challenge doesn't matter. Maybe you want to overcome stubbornness, be nice to the in-laws, learn to ride a bike, reduce your carbon footprint, build up a savings account, send your kid to college or learn a sport. No matter the challenges in life, big or small, they all matter and it is important to work to overcome them all. If you let the challenges in life keep you down, it is pretty difficult to take this book to heart. Most things we seek to overcome aren't the huge battles. They are the saving money and losing five-pounds variety. But when it comes to living your life, they are just as important to overcome.

I guarantee you, even if you can't think of anything right now, there

is something in your life you can overcome – right
that.

Oftentimes it is *you* that needs to be overco
attitude, your time management or your pre-conc..
are things you need to overcome. Sometimes it is outside factoi.
your boss or your in-laws, but those still can be internal corrections
that need to be made in order to overcome the challenge in front of
you. Take some time to evaluate some of these things. One way is to
consider things that maybe aren't going your way right now, but instead
of looking for external explanations, find ways that you yourself could
be the problem – and therefore, also the solution. If you don't have a
high credit score, it is not the fault of CitiBank or where you bought
that iPod, but rather maybe it's your spending habits. Looking inward
can be hard, especially if you aren't used to being honest with yourself.
If that is the case though, you might be amazed at what you could learn
about yourself from others around you. They see things about you to
which you might be completely blind!

An exercise developed by Joseph Luft and Harry Ingham back in
1955, *Jahari Window*, can help you explore your true self. In its simplest
form, it uses 56 positive adjectives and you select six that most describe
you. Then a group of your peers select six they think represent you. At
that point, they are mapped out into four quadrants. If both sides select
the same word, it shows that everyone is aware of that character trait.
If you select a word but your peers don't it is said to be a *façade* because
your peers don't see it in you. If it is a trait you want, you will need to
work to bring that out into the open. If your peers put words down
and you don't, those are called, *blind spots*. You don't see them because
they are blind spots to you but they are coming through to your peers.
The fourth and final quadrant is the *unknown* and if neither party uses
words then they fall here and they either don't apply or neither side is
aware of the trait.

This activity can help you eliminate your own personal blindness
and help you learn about yourself and areas you may need to be stronger in. The two areas for reflection thus far in this chapter relate to

nding who the authentic you truly is. Not only can these ques-
and this activity help you understand a little bit more about you,
knowing how others see you can help you overcome yourself!

REFLECTIONS

If you had to describe yourself in 2-3 words, what words would you choose?

Are those the same words your family, friends, co-workers, and acquaintances would use to describe you? If not, you need to work to merge the two "yous."

I felt like a normal kid growing up. I liked to play in the sandbox. I liked to play with Hot Wheels and on occasion (when forced by my sister) I did play with Barbie's. Not until I reached middle school did I start to feel different. Most of my guy friends were becoming interested in girls, but I wasn't. I felt like an outsider. Only 13, I couldn't put my finger on it. As the next few years went on, I started to realize that I was not only not attracted to girls, but I was attracted to guys. It was frightening to me and I hated it. I cried. I prayed. I thought about ending my life. I thought anything would be easier than living with this. I hated doing it, but I asked a girl to prom. I wanted to go to the dance but still didn't understand the emotions I was feeling. As I went to college, I even asked a girl out, but she turned me down. It wasn't until midway through my junior year of college when I finally started to come to terms with the fact that I was, in fact, gay.

When I started telling a few of my friends that I was gay, I was a nervous wreck. My hands would get clammy and I would physically shake every time I shared my deepest, darkest secret. There isn't even a word for what I was feeling. I feared rejection. I feared hatred. I feared being hit in the face. I distinctly remember taking a road trip to see Asitha because I wanted to tell him in person. I'd written it all down in case I got there and couldn't tell him by myself. I'm glad I did because I couldn't talk when I got there. As he read my letter, he reached out and held my hand in his. When he finished reading, he said, "Okay, you have to give me a hug now." Much to my surprise, everyone took it well and each time I gathered up the courage to tell another friend, I still prepared for the worst.

Each time someone told me it was okay and they still loved me, it affirmed that it was okay to be me. It reiterated my belief that I was okay the way I was. It brought me out of my own personal hell and helped me to start living my life once again. Since that age of 13, I had lived two lives, one everyone saw, and the one that only I knew and only vaguely understood. Even with each positive reaction, I still feared the prospect of rejection. I feared the anger. I feared losing someone I cared about. In this world, it's still tough being gay. It's even tougher when you're a conservative Lutheran living in a small Midwestern town that still believes *gay* is a bad word.

My challenge was not to correct this about myself; it was a much broader need to live my life openly, confidently and without fear. It wasn't until June 2006, six months after I graduated from college that I did start living that way. I came out to my parents on June 17, and it went like I thought it would. They were unhappy and at the time, unwilling to accept it. Even though I predicted that would be their response, I knew I had to tell them the truth. I needed to overcome the fear of being me and remaining in the closet was the last thing holding me back. Now I had told everyone close to me and while most of the reactions went much better than expected, it's still something I have to overcome on a daily basis. *Why?* It's pretty simple actually: I live in a world that is still intolerant and scared of who I am. I get up every morning and I know that just because I overcame my own fears doesn't mean I still don't have to work to overcome other people and the world around me. While most of the United States still doesn't recognize the rights of gay and lesbian people, let alone allow for a legal form of marriage or civil unions, some things are changing. Employment non-discrimination and anti-bullying laws for students have passed. In the fall of 2009, President Obama signed the Matthew Shepard Act which made, after ten years of political maneuvering, any crime committed based on someone's sexuality a hate crime and thus prosecutable by the U.S. Justice Department. Despite everything, I know overcoming the world and myself is something I can do. I know it because I'm doing it every day by simply living my life openly and full of passion. My parents are even starting to come around.

I am a person who loves life and loves exploring what that means with everyone around me. Someday I will be a father and do the soccer-dad thing, although I actually hope my child plays tennis or football. I dare to become a father despite society saying I can't be a good one or shouldn't even raise a child. Every time I go to a coffee shop, I smile when I see a father and his kid sharing a Saturday coffee and juice. I dream about the day when I get to do the same. I dared myself to overcome a great obstacle and I am better for it. Even my friends are better for it because coming out forced them to question themselves and their own opinions. By simply being me, I allowed others question themselves and overcome their own fears and prejudices.

The best part of this story is the moral: You are who you are. Be not afraid. Every day that you challenge yourself to be better is a service to yourself and those around you.

Acknowledging that you indeed have something to overcome is the first step. When you recognize there is something you'd like to change, the next step is daring yourself to do it! Do something about it. Take action. Remember, you are the director of your life so take control of it. Chances are you will be energized by just dreaming of overcoming your obstacle which will empower you to take the steps necessary to beat your obstacle.

There are times of course where you're not going to be able to do it by yourself. You're not always going to be able to overcome your challenge without some help. In these instances, it is okay to use the word "not." It's okay to go up to someone and say, "I can't do this alone. Will you please help me?" Abraham Lincoln had a great team around him and he wasn't afraid to ask them for advice. He was notorious for having late-night fireside chats with friends and foes alike. People battling cancer oftentimes have to ask for help with their daily lives whether cooking a meal or watering their plants while they undergo treatment. I had to ask my friends for their shoulders to cry on when my battle reached its peak. As much as overcoming obstacles is up to you, many times you will not be the only person involved. Your battle includes your loved ones, your co-workers and your friends. Asking for help is often needed. That's not a sign of weakness or is it an impulse you need to change. It's a sign of courage, strength, and your dedication to making a better you.

REFLECTIONS

What is something in your life that you can overcome today?

What is something you'd like to overcome, but don't believe you can?

What can you do to start overcoming the challenge listed in question two today?

When asked what the secret to success was, sales guru Og Mandino said, "You should triple your rate of failure." It applies to life perfectly. You have to fail. You have to constantly work to overcome every challenge and road-block in your life. You can't quit. You have to keep going and keep living your life to its fullest. Anything is possible and when you dare to overcome the things blocking your dream life, those failures are absolutely worth it.

Points to Remember

» Know who you are and be sure your peers see that side of you 100 percent of the time. Be the authentic you.

» Overcoming yourself may be your biggest obstacle to overcome.

» If you can't overcome an obstacle, at least don't let it overtake and control you. You can still control your emotions, thoughts and attitude.

» A failure only happens when you decide to give up.

» Live your life openly, confidently and without fear.

» Every day that you challenge yourself to be better is a service to yourself and those around you.

» Sometimes you may need to ask for help when you're facing challenges. It's a sign of courage and your dedication to making a better you.

Chapter 7

Chase Your Passion

"THE QUESTION ISN'T WHO IS GOING TO LET
ME; IT'S WHO IS GOING TO STOP ME."

-Ayn Rand

I believe in order to live a completely fulfilling life you must be willing to do anything to live your passions. These are the things that get your blood flowing and can turn a gloomy day into the best day. Chasing after something you wholeheartedly love and enjoy feeds your soul and can open up new doors of opportunity you never knew existed. If you believe anything is possible, then chasing your passions should be easy. The passions are yours and you get to decide what that means, how much time you want to spend and how much energy you want to put into whatever you are passionate about.

One of my many passions is writing. It wasn't always that way, but as I reached high school, I enjoyed writing while others simply just enjoyed life. That's not to say that I didn't enjoy my life too. But most of my enjoyment came from writing. I enjoy the process of writing; taking my thoughts from a random idea to a concrete, well thought out creation. My senior year of high school I wrote for the school newspaper, covering sports, news and writing a column. I toiled around with short stories. I even wrote speeches as if I'd become president. I also spent a lot of time reading, not just for enjoyment but to learn how others wrote. During my first year of college at North Iowa Area Community College, I became an even better writer. I wrote personality profiles and informative news pieces for our school newspaper, *LOGOS*. When I reached the University of Northern Iowa, I joined the sports writing team of *The Northern Iowan*, where I pitched story ideas to my editor that would give the student body and sports fans a better look at our student athletes. The best part for me came from the ability to create the stories and see the results of my hard work.

While at Northern Iowa, I also wrote a 26 chapter story that I posted online. I had found the place online years before where writers from all over the world posted stories for the world to read. I decided I wanted to try my hand at a long, novel-like story. I wrote about a high school athlete who is privately dealing with coming to realize that he is gay. Not only did the process teach me a lot, but I had the opportunity in the creation of the story to explore some personal issues I was going through at the time.

Once I decided to write this book, I just did it. It was not as easy as just sitting down and writing though. The fact is I had to make a plan. Once I felt good about my outline and direction after fleshing out the concept, I felt ready to go. This was almost a year-long process – before I even started the introduction! I built a writing schedule that allowed me to finish the first draft in less than two months. I spent a lot of time at coffee houses – another one of my passions. Most of all, I have a passion for people. Writing this book has helped me explore myself and other people. Not to mention the fact that it has allowed me to help you explore yours.

One of the most impactful things anyone has ever asked me was, "What have you done to achieve your dreams today?" That was the first time anyone had ever asked me something like that and to be honest, I had never given it much thought. In fact, I never thought of it in those terms. The question itself forced me to look at what I truly had passions for and what really energized me. I had never been asked. I had a college degree and I enjoyed the work I was doing, but it didn't get my blood pumping. My life didn't have that feeling of exhilaration and the life-affirming purpose I believe we all look for and seek. One of the first things that came to mind was quite simple: I loved speaking in front of groups.

From that day, I began the process of chasing that passion. As I started to research what I wanted to do with my speaking, I figured out I wanted to be a motivational speaker and leadership and life trainer. The first step was creating a company. Today that company is Richard Dedor Communications, and while I only have one employee (myself), I am proud because on that day I started chasing my love. Since this journey began in 2007, I have been fortunate enough to work with a wide range of clients and have spoken in front of hundreds of people. But it's more than that. Every day I have the amazing privilege to share my experiences with people all across the world. This journey is a labor of love and because of that I'm not going to stop. I try to ask myself everyday what I'm doing to achieve my dreams. It helps to keep me moving forward towards my other goals associated with this passion and my overall zest for life.

Passions can come in many shapes and sizes. Like I said, I have many. My biggest ones are writing, speaking and learning. Some other things I find energy from include coffee, tennis and working out. I believe each person in this world has at least one passion. I recently spoke at an event in St. Louis and one of the women in attendance had recently taken the option of retirement and I asked her what she was going to do with her free time. She immediately lit up and said, "I'm going to talk!" We kept talking and she explained that she plans on helping other people in her former professional get better at their jobs. She's a woman who worked for 40 years, had the passion, and is going to keep at it only in a different capacity. The things that drive your soul, that energize you can be as simple as reading and as wide and broad as changing the world.

REFLECTIONS

What are some of your passions? What brings you true joy?

PASSIONS NEVER DIE

No matter the sport, athletes are notoriously passionate people. They have to be. In order to play at a high level and to be willing to dedicate so much time and energy takes an extremely high level of passion and commitment. Sometimes passion just happens and sometimes it grows over time. Once you feel it, you just have to see where it goes. If there is something you want to go after, you should. In all honesty, you don't have to have a passion to start, because just by going after it, it may start to develop on its own. An athlete is passionate because they found something to be passionate about. That's what happened with me and tennis. No one in my family played or even watched the sport. One day I picked up a racquet and I was hooked. It's no different than artists, entertainers, writers or teachers. Passion knows no boundaries. Passion is not only what drives an athlete, but it is certainly what fuels them to finish and to compete in the first place; to challenge and tackle every obstacle, moment, line and swing.

To be successful you have to learn from every challenge. While most challenges incorporate factors outside your control, part of every battle in life is going to be with yourself and your attitude. Your success will revolve around how much you continue to learn about yourself and your craft. I will never say that passion is all you need. But I also don't believe that pure talent or, muscles, or effort is enough alone. You have to want it badly enough. It's that strong passion that makes you love it more and chase it harder, no matter the circumstances.

Mike Shanahan is a perfect example of having to change the focus of his passion. Mike is a guy who lives and breathes football. As an undersized quarterback at Eastern Illinois University, he got hit pretty hard during a routine play but felt fine immediately afterwards. By the time he arrived at his apartment after the game he started urinating blood. He was rushed to the emergency room where it was found that his kidney had been split in half. The situation was so critical that they issued his last-rights because the doctors didn't believe he would survive. In a stroke of good fortune and possibly of dreams to come, he survived. He made it and today is one of the most successful coaches in the National Football League. That day changed his path forever but not his passion. He lost the ability to compete on a field, but remarkably, refused to let that destroy his love for football. Mike's story is known to most football fans, but what is often overlooked is that once he found out he would never strap on football pads again but he vowed to become the best coach he could.

Mike quickly impressed his fellow coaches by his work ethic and his drive to be successful. One time he sent a coach to re-draw a play because the X's and O's weren't drawn perfectly. He worked his way up to an NFL head coach very quickly and his first head coaching job was with the Oakland Raiders. Four games into his second year at the helm, he was very publically fired. After that experience, he went to work under one of the best coaches and teachers football has seen in the last fifty years in Bill Walsh. After a few years under Bill's tutelage, Mike was given the reins of the Denver Broncos. In three years he turned around a fledgling organization and led them to back-to-back Super Bowl wins. His résumé is glowing with three Super Bowl wins, two of them as head coach. Mike is an example of a guy who was dealt a terrible hand and had his love taken away from him. But what he did, what he learned from his accident was that there are countless ways to chase your passion and keep it a central part of your life.

After I graduated from college, I started to play more and more tennis. I was living near my friend Tylor who always wanted to hit around. Through our practices, my love for tennis reignited. I played more tournaments that summer than ever before. We both scheduled our last tournament for August that fall. We played at different skill levels so we promised to meet up for dinner at the end of the first day. By the time I made it to the restaurant, I was in quite a bit of pain. I could hardly walk. I can still picture it today as I shuffled my feet as I walked, barely moving my back due to the pain I was in. Sitting in the restaurant was excruciating, as was the walk back to my car an hour later. I tried to play through it, but a few months of trying that put me in an MRI tube to find out why the pain wouldn't go away. Multiple trips and tests later, I was told I needed to reduce how much I played because my lower back bones were becoming compressed and causing a fluid buildup.

It killed me to stop playing but because it was so painful to play, I had to. But I didn't stop watching and talking tennis. I didn't stop studying the game's best players. I didn't sell or throw away my equipment. I have spent a lot of time off the court and I've made a personal vow to enter a few tournaments in 2010. I'm coming back. I'm going to give it my best shot. I know what my passion is and I've spent time getting my body recovered and in better shape. My point is that once you have a passion, it never really leaves you – it's connected to you for life and no matter what obstacles get in your way, there is always a way to keep it a part of you.

Of course going after something you enjoy can have rough moments. Mike had to change his focus and be fired while I had to endure injuries and take time off. I had many moments where I considered selling off all my tennis equipment and finding something new to spend my energy and time on. But tennis is in my blood. Tennis and me go hand in hand. Going through these struggles requires you to keep a positive attitude about yourself and reminds you why you spend so much time doing it. There are two basic reasons you chase your passions and they relate to rewards: intrinsic and extrinsic. Most times our reasons for doing things will be intrinsically motivated. These are rewards we create for ourselves. Extrinsic rewards are those determined and awarded by someone else. On the other hand, the rewards we give ourselves are intrinsic and mean something to only us. This more times than not is the real motivating factor behind what we do with our passions. Whatever your rewards for yourself, they must provide positive reinforcement.

REFLECTIONS

Think back for your entire life. What are some passions you had that you let go of and didn't do anything about?

If throughout this chapter so far, you are having trouble locating a true passion of yours or are realizing what you think is a true passion really isn't, don't fret. Like I said before, I believe every person has a least one if not many things that engage and excite them. My job here is to find yours and cultivate you through to action. Hopefully so far you've been able to look at your passions and are beginning to see and understand what drives you.

FROM PASSION TO ACTION!

Alright, so you have a passion – *now what?* Once you know something you are passionate about, it is time for the action stage. It is time to do something about it. It is time to make it a part of who you are. In the very least, you must give it a try and see if you do in fact enjoy it. I had always wanted to paint but I also constantly told myself I didn't have the skills. It's funny how as people who are supposed to believe in ourselves, how we often talk down to ourselves. We do it more than the people around us. That was definitely me when it came to painting! It was me stopping me and the last chapter focused on daring you to overcome the obstacles in your life. This chapter focuses on once you overcome them, how to go about chasing the things you're passionate about.

It wasn't simple but over the course of a few months, I researched painting and then one day decided that I was just going to do it. I went out, found an easel, brushes, paint and canvases and just started. Putting the first glob of paint on that first canvas was a scary experience and I struggled because I had no idea what to do. I have never had an art class in my life but I have overcome that fear and overcome myself and just did it. I grew tired of having a passion for art and not doing anything about it. I decided to go after painting because *what good is having a passion for something if you are not living it and making it a part of you?* Some will argue that just because you have a passion, it does not mean you have to become that passion. I agree. But for instance, if you have a passion for painting, who is to say you can't visit a museum every month, become a docent, or write a book about your favorite piece of art or artist?

In regards to my paintings, I'm not going to lie and say I'm a brilliant painter today. It is still a struggle when I pick up the paintbrush, but I'm doing it. I have a lot to learn and while I don't have any inkling of becoming the next Picasso, or even a distant relative, I'm enjoying the journey of discovering this newfound passion. It is important not to quit something right away. I could have quit when I nervously picked up the brush for the first time. But I just started and let my imagination run wild. There are going to be passions you have that are going to be a struggle for you right from the start. You are going to fail and you are going to have to fight the urge to quit. But you can't let any amount of failure get in the way of doing something you might actually enjoy. It's because I started to chase this passion that I've been in one local art show and had some of my work displayed in a local coffee shop. Chasing after something you're excited about has many ups and downs. You will fail. But you will also succeed if you don't let yourself quit.

REFLECTIONS

What do you need to be successful?

How can you reward yourself along the way?

What short-term goals can you set for yourself to guide you on your quest to chase your passions?

I used to love to do Lite-Brite and until recently had given up all hopes of ever becoming a world-renowned extraordinaire in that exquisite field. By the time I turned 11 years old, my rewards for the Lite-Brite had gone away. However, upon picking up the newspaper one Sunday morning, I read about artist Mark Beekman of Pennsylvania who created a five-and-a-half by eleven foot rendering of the famous Last Supper painting.[1] Did I mention he made it with a Lite-Brite? It took over 15 months to construct and contained 124,418 pegs! Apparently this astounding feat has created a rush of competition for the record of largest Lite-Brite creation as it has since been surpassed by an even larger Lite-Brite creation. My point is simple: You are only limited by your willingness, or lack thereof, to chase your passion.

History doesn't judge by how much you accomplish in life but on how you spend your days. *Have you impacted the lives of those around you?* A common exercise is to write your own eulogy so you can think about what you want it to say. It is a way to figure out what you want to have accomplished by the time your life is complete. It's a great exercise but I want you to think about something else even more. Instead of what you want in your eulogy, *what do you want other people to say about you?* We will all have different answers to that question, but I do know that what will be said about you won't be praise for how many hours you worked each work, how much money you made, what your IQ score was, or what your GPA was in college. Rather, what people say about you will be the final answer to this question: *Have you truly lived?* Mark Beekman absolutely dared to chase his passion. In his story, his passion was Lite-Brite art. He created a magnificent work of art from a child's toy. Your passions have no limits or deadlines. *But why wait?* Beekman didn't have any limitations and simply lived his passion out loud.

ELIMINATE NO POSSIBILITIES

If you can dream it, then it has to be possible. In today's ever-connected world, finding information and networking with people all over the world has become very easy and because of this constantly changing medium, you now have the ability to find new avenues for your dreams. One of the great things about the Internet is how easy it is to stay in touch with people. This probably has less to do with how much we care about them and really about how easy communicating instantly with practically everyone has become. It has also opened up doors to finding new relationships that just a few years ago would have taken a direct contact to establish. With various connections all across the country, I have been able to communicate with authors and speakers and people just interested in creating the impossible dream they have. It's always energizing to speak with people who are living their dream and helping others do the same.

One such connection for me is author Chris Amisano. By the time we connected through a mutual friend, he had already published one book, *An Imperfect Arrangement*, and was finishing his second. I quickly started to pick his brain on how to write and publish a book, and on my tough days while I was writing this book, I even vented to him. Having been where I am and now a full-time freelance marketer and writer, he said these words: "As far as advice, I would have to say just don't get frustrated, because this is something I do every single day. I would also say to enjoy it. I have to remind myself on the hard days that I chose this to get a kick out of working."

We all know the old adage about how to have a great career is "find what you love and then find someone who will pay you to do it." That's what I'm doing now. I'm writing because I love it. I speak because I love it. And yes, this dream I am chasing will be tough. But the joys received from chasing this passion and living the impossible are much more rewarding than wondering and playing the wondering game.

Life is meant to be lived and the best way to make that happen is to know your passions and to then chase them. Do it. Join the chase! No one can do it but you.

REFLECTIONS

What has been holding you back?

What can you do in the next week to take action on one of your passions that is dormant?

A friend of mine from high school, Ryan Borcherding, attended to the University of California – Los Angeles to study acting. In high school, everyone knew he would one day win Emmys and Oscars. He performed every chance he had. More than that, he lived it. He shared his passion for theatre with anyone who would listen. He helped build a traveling high school theatre group. Everything in his life revolved around his passion for acting. While at UCLA, he also found a passion for spreading theatre to the world through work in countries like Ghana and Turkey. While still in college Ryan traveled to Ghana to work with an organization called "Theatre for a Change" in a chronically impoverished area of the country. His mission during his time there was to help the local community tell their stories through theatre. He came to find that they had stories deeply rooted in their own experiences about the threats to their lives and families.

Returning from Ghana, Ryan finished his degree and soon pursued another opportunity to spread his love of theatre in Turkey to help local artists develop short plays with the hope that they would be able to perform them for the community. When I asked him about his experiences, he said to me, "I'm enjoying it immensely." How many people can honestly say that? That's what comes from chasing your passion! I'm fortunate to call him a friend and he continually inspires me through his dedication to his passion. Through his unique approach to changing the world, he is inspiring hope around the globe, one community at a time. Ryan simply knew his passion, tried everything related to it and found his niche of where he wanted to spend his time and energy with the theatre.

Everything must remain a possibility. Every moment of every day is a chance for you to cultivate one of your passions. It is a chance to ask questions and learn a little more each day. When Mike Shanahan couldn't play anymore, he understood football gave him enjoyment, so he found another way to remain involved in the sport. Everything is a possibility and every door an opportunity.

I have also begun to cultivate a passion for photography. While it adds stress to an already stressful life, I enjoy the chance to capture a moment in time – to freeze the frames for one split second and have others experience that moment over and over. Anytime I take on a new passion, I want to do well. That desire to do well means I have to be willing to fail. The potential failure and the desire to do well usually increases stress. While I still feel like I only know one-tenth of a percent of all there is to know about photography, I am enjoying the journey of discovery. I am chasing dreams and passions. I have even risen before the sunrise in the bitter cold to take photos of the sunrise – not for any prize but just because I wanted to do it and capture that moment.

Back in *Chapter 1*, you examined the focus areas of your life. Now look at it from the side of what your passions are and what you want them to be. If your focus areas don't reflect these passions then you need to readjust the key focus areas of your life so that you have the time and energy to spend on your passions.

You can overcome obstacles, big and small, no matter what! If you know yourself and you are truly open to changing your attitude, you are free to believe in yourself and your passions. It is a liberating thought and a joyous achievement. Dare to chase your passions. No one else will do it for you and no one will be able to experience your life for you. Only you can feel the ball in your hand. Only you can sing out loud. Only you can inspire others. Only you can live out loud. Chase your passions. I dare you!

PASSIONS FEED THE SOUL

The top sports story of 2006, as judged by ESPN's *SportsCenter*, was the story of Jason McElwain. As a senior at Greece Athena High School in Rochester, N.Y., he served as the basketball manager for the boys' varsity team. Jason never played in a game and was never in the box score, but he worked every game and assisted at every practice. Jason lived and breathed basketball, and it lived and breathed him. After all, it was his passion. The reason Jason never played in a game is because he is autistic. Though he wasn't in a jersey, he became as much a part of the team as the captain. He would stay late after practice to shoot around, probably dreaming of making that tie-breaking three-pointer to win a championship. Before the last home game of his senior year, the coach called him into his office and told him that in the final home game, Jason would don a jersey with the rest of the team. Imagine that! The coach decided to dress a guy who had never made a basket because he had never been in a game, but he had also never been given the shot. With four minutes to go in the game, the coach sent Jason in. In moments, the first pass from a teammate came his way and he quickly shot and missed. The next trip down the floor he shot again but with the same result. It began to seem that the dream to see points next to his name was slipping through his fingers. Finally, almost unbelievably, Jason threw up a three-pointer with a perfect arch that soared through the round, orange rim. Three points! What happened next seemed once improbable and now not only possible, but happening right in front of everyone's eyes in the stands.

Over the final four minutes, Jason became the highest scorer of the game. At the end of the game, he was carted off the court on his teammates' shoulders. A champion on the court; an inspiration to everyone.

What is so incredible about Jason's story isn't that after four years of managing the team he finally had his dream of playing realized. It is simply that he lived and breathed his passion for no other reason than because he loved it. Jason was never going to make it to the NBA as a player and maybe not even as a manager. But his story demonstrates that people who chase and believe in their passions can inspire the world. Yes he did score 18 points, but Jason's success lies in his dedication to practicing on his own and always staying involved with the team. Through his passion he showed children affected with autism that even with the disease, you can still live your passions and achieve great things.

An article on ESPN.com said:[2] "There are thousands of families across the country, getting a diagnosis of autism for their 3-year-old; they look at Jason and have tears in their eyes," said Dr. Susan Hyman, an associate professor for pediatrics at the University of Rochester's Strong Center for Developmental Disabilities. "Because the image they have in their minds isn't of some strapping young teenager making baskets from half court. The hope and the promise this provides -- it's priceless."

While Jason's story is about overcoming an obstacle, it becomes more about him never quitting on his love for basketball that matters the most. Jason dared to chase his passion and through that, he is daring others to do the same because of what becomes possible when you do.

By now you know I love my work as a public speaker. Oddly enough though, there are moments when I can be extremely shy and introverted. All through school, when I would meet someone new it was difficult for me to start conversations. It's also funny because when I am around my best friends, I won't stop talking, but when I get around my family I'm much quieter and much more reserved. From the moment I would get in front of a class to give a speech in school, I felt at home. I am comfortable, I'm at ease and I'm able to easily connect with people. Even with my introverted nature in school, I was able to find that I enjoyed speaking and it quickly became my passion. My classmates hated me because I became good at giving speeches and would always volunteer to go first in class, thus setting the bar too high for everyone else.

Anyone who finds their passion and lives it knows the feeling that comes when engaging in it. Being on stage or leading a workshop fires up my energy and my passion for life. It's much like the same excitement that comes from playing or watching tennis. Those two things fire up my soul and push me to keep going after my passions.

Aside from all these stories and practical applications, there is one overriding key to your success when it comes to chasing the things you are most passionate. Whether you need to start a company, quit your job, or just travel the world, you must surround yourself with the best team of *thrivers* you can find. When you build a team around you that rewards and supports you, they will not let you fail. They help you keep your eyes on your dream. It works for me and I know it will work for you.

┌───┐
│ **REFLECTIONS**   │
│ *Who is on your team of thrivers?*   │
│   │
│   │
└───┘

When Beethoven lost his hearing, it didn't make him stop. In fact, it was then that he truly started to listen to music. He suffered from tinnitus which made it difficult for him to appreciate music. It was at this time he wrote his Heiligenstadt Testament, a letter to his brothers about his resolution that, despite his hearing loss; he was going to continue living for his music. In part, he wrote: "[…] only art it was that withheld me, ah it seemed impossible to leave the world until I had produced all that I felt called upon me to produce, and so I endured this wretched existence – truly wretched, an excitable body which a sudden change can throw from the best into the worst state […]"[3]

He kept composing and learned new ways to create his art. It is said that at the premiere of his Ninth Symphony, he had to be turned around to see the applause of the audience. Even though he couldn't hear the applause or even hear the true power of his piece, he kept creating.

I truly believe that if you have a passion for something, the only thing holding you back from doing something about it will be you. Whether it's my painting, or Beethoven's music, passions must remain in your focus at all times. Chasing your passion means setting realistic goals in line with your talents or handicaps, but to dream big at the same time. You must set expectations for success on your terms, not others'. It remains your life and success can be just doing it, or it could be selling a painting or starting a theatre program in Turkey. When it comes to believing anything is possible, the answer lies in chasing your passions.

Points to Remember

» You must be willing to do anything to live your passion

» Ask yourself every day, "What have I done to achieve my dreams today?"

» You have to want your dream badly enough. Having that strong desire for your passion will make you chase it harder, no matter the circumstances.

» The struggles along the way require you to keep a positive attitude about yourself and your dream.

» You are only limited by your own willingness to chase your passion.

» If you can dream it, then it has to be possible.

» Passions feed the soul.

» Build a team of thrivers around you.

Chapter 8

Be a Lifelong Learner

"LEARNING IS NOT ACHIEVED BY CHANCE,
IT MUST BE SOUGHT FOR WITH ARDOR AND
ATTENDED TO WITH DILIGENCE."

-Abigail Adams

In order to graduate from my high school, I had to prove I had learned six things through my four years. Forget math, science and government; my graduation depended on demonstrating my advancement on six pillars of learning. A week before I was to graduate, I presented to an Acacemic Advisor how over four years I had grown and integrated the six pillars into my life. Think about it – after passing all my exams, ducking the circus of senior photos and commencement attire, and faced with looming family fun, the last thing any high school student wants to do is demonstrate that they have learned. On top of that I had to take the ACT test twice. Of course, the threat of not graduating is even more potent senior year and I succinctly sat down to do what was necessary and appease the powers that be.

After all that stress and hard work and the best of intentions from the school board, I can honestly say that I only remember one of the six pillars. The only thing I can recall is the theme for this chapter: lifelong learning. I had to show through academics and my work in the community that I was living the pillars. In addition, I had to support the argument that in order to be a valuable resource to society, I must be a lifelong learner. Even back then, I believed it to be true, despite how much I didn't want to have to prove it to my Academic Advisor.

When it comes to this subject, I believe there are two types of learners in this world: those who embrace it and those who don't. For example, people who get up, go to work, eat lunch, desperately chug an afternoon coffee, battle the rush-hour traffic, arrive home in time to have a rushed dinner, check the kids' homework, watch a little television, maybe read that morning's paper and exhaustedly crawl into bed, don't appear to embrace learning. But there is nothing wrong with that person. They still learn throughout their day. Where it becomes a problem is when that becomes the routine for today, tomorrow, the next day and the next. They may learn new skills at their job; how to cook a better meal and maybe they even learn a new hobby. The key here is that this person isn't excited about it and they certainly aren't excited or looking for ways to apply new skills and knowledge in all facets of their lives.

On the opposite site of the learning spectrum are people who may do the same things as the first person, but they also constantly seeking more knowledge. These people constantly read, study and question the leading thinkers in their fields. They are the ones writing papers, researching other avenues for their companies and their families. It is these people who have embraced fully the idea of becoming a lifelong learner. Aside from seeking new information, they have a positive and welcoming attitude to everything new in their lives. That is the profound difference between the two. It's about attitude. It's about having a willingness to apply it and volunteer it freely to those around you.

While there are days I know I can fall into the group that isn't focused on applying new skills in my life, I know I don't stay there for long because I am definitely a passionate learner. Again, that remains the key point of being a successful lifelong learner. I absolutely love learning. It inspires me and challenges me. I know that by continually seeking knowledge that I will open doors that were not open before. I also must admit that I admire those who are smarter than I and can retain more information. Other people, my best friends included, are able to learn quicker than I, but I don't let that deter me. I work at my own speed and so should you. Don't compare yourself with others. Your knowledge is for you to experience, so long as you remain passionate and excited about the process, good things will happen.

REFLECTIONS

Think about the last week of your life. What learning occurred in your life during the last week? Make a list of all the things you learned. Was the learning intentional or unintentional?

Noted American psychologist, author, inventor, advocate for social reform and poet B. F. Skinner spent his career researching the best way to teach children and the impact of psychology in learning.[1] Through all his studies and experiences with his own family, Skinner found there are five main obstacles people have when it comes to learning. Of these, the fear of learning and not having enough positive reinforcement stand out the most. First of all, you will fail. But a lifelong learner takes every stumble for what it really is: a learning opportunity. In fact, when learning something new, you have nothing to lose. So you don't learn it. So what? But if you really want to learn it, you will find a way.

Additionally, Skinner posts five basic teaching principles including: repeat the directions as many times as possible and give positive reinforcement. Beginning with the latter, I have tried to focus throughout this book on the *positives* not only associated with being passionate and going after your dreams, but the *positives* that come from failure. As far as repeating the directions as many times as possible, I bet if you go back through this book, you will see that I repeated, almost ad nauseam the phrase "anything is possible." There is a reason for that and it's because the more I repeat it and ingrain it into your mind, the likelier it is to stick. I have, through my repetition, built a pathway to help you achieve your dreams.

It not only works for you individually, but if you help others in their learning by teaching step-by-step things you already know and utilize positive reinforcement along the way, you aid the learning journeys of others and empower them to expand their own knowledge.

LEARN

I remember a few months ago I was reading my latest book at my favorite local coffee house (a random "library pick off the shelf because I liked the cover"), and I by the time I neared the end I started crying. Not loud thankfully, but silently letting the words of the story affect me in such a way that I let my guard down. I wiped away my tears and looked up hoping no one was staring at me. In that moment I couldn't help but notice how their lives continued on around me, oblivious to my emotional appearance. A father and his young daughter caught my eye. He had his coffee and she had her juice. It was a Saturday afternoon. Even though I was still wiping away tears, I smiled. For me, the father and his daughter provided living proof that you can always learn from someone. They made me smile. He was probably some big business man, in jeans and a t-shirt with his daughter in a coffeehouse. More importantly, I noticed he didn't pull out his smart phone. He sat there and played with his daughter. Just from those two minutes, I learned two lessons: something is always around to make you smile and keep your eyes up and focused on the moment right in front of you. That's the kind of learning I'm talking about. Everyone around you can teach you something every moment of every day. It's not exclusive to books, studies, reports, training sessions and classes. Life teaches us. You just have to listen and be open to anything that comes your way.

I try every day to be not only a lifelong learner, but someone who teach those around me just by following my example. Whenever I talk to people, I am always listening. I listen for their story, their personal challenges and triumphs and if I might have some brilliant experience to relate to them. But the most important part of listening to someone is the knowledge you are likely to gain about them. You have an avenue into their soul. When we talk and share our stories and knowledge, we share something that is personal to us. From one small tale, there is much you can gather and apply to your own life. *What lesson did they learn? What lesson do you take from it that you can apply to your own life?* When you realize that not only can you help by sharing your knowledge, but you can learn from others in everyday situations, you open yourself to a lot of opportunities. Each and every one of you has learned a lesson in your life from which someone else can take their own lessons.

Look at the stories of the elderly who go back to college after they retire. I have seen numerous accounts throughout the years on the news about seniors who never got their diploma or didn't have the chance to go to college as a young adult. Some go back because they want something to do and learning is a natural choice. Others go back because they want to achieve their goal of graduating from high school or college. Whatever the reason, they are amazing examples of lifelong learners. Just off Interstate 71 in Cincinnati, Ohio, there is a school called the *Retirement University*. They specialize in pre-retirement classes designed to prepare future retirees for their new lives. At the University of Toulouse in southern France, there is a focus not just on learning, but improving the quality of life. At Toulouse there is a college for the elderly called the University of the Third Age. The program has no minimum age requirement and has been in existence since 1974. Their goal is to "improve the psychological, social and intellectual quality of the lives of older people by using the resources of a major university and integrating these students [...] into its life."[2]

These elderly students are taking it upon themselves to seek more knowledge, to keep learning and growing. But it isn't just book learning, it's life learning. It's about sharing experiences and growing from others. When you learn just to learn, you are quietly growing as a person. In a 2006 article in *AARP Magazine*, writer Rosabeth Moss Kanter discussed a project she was working on to create a generation of community activists.[3] She said, "It's using school to move forward." Her plan, based on statistics showing that Americans aged 50 to 70 are expressing an increasing interest in community service, is to serve as a teaching ground for local, national and international service projects. For the Baby Boomers, it's not just about retirement anymore. It is about service learning. They serve to learn about themselves and also about others. This journey allows them to serve others while they are learning. Having an open mind to all avenues that provide knowledge is the key to learning. These elderly students and activists continue to serve as an example to everyone about the importance of learning for today and tomorrow. They also show us that learning never stops.

I hope that when I am 70, I will have written a few books, given a few thousand speeches, have grandchildren, be retired, and still seek out new things to discover. Maybe by that time I will get around to shark diving!

It is often said that decisions are made by those who show up. *Are you going to be the person with the answers, or the person with your hands in your pockets? And, if you don't have the answers will you seek them out?* In truth, seeking out answers to your questions and taking the unknown path has much more to do with lifelong learning than just being the one with the answers. Think about it this way – if you already think you have the answer, *will you challenge yourself to discover more?* Sometimes we think we know so much that we forget how much there is still to learn. Even beyond that, we too often think of the answer as the destination, completely forgetting how vibrant and invigorating the journey is. You may know that Beijing is the capital of China, but have you ever thought how much more you could learn and experience by going and finding out?

The daily routine I mentioned earlier has a lot more players in it than just you. Purposefully surrounding yourself with people who want to seek more out of life has a huge impact on you as well. Think about the people you know. *Do you surround yourself with people who just learn by circumstance, or is your office-mate someone who jumps at the chance to learn and helps you learn new things as well?* I will agree that it is scary to put yourself in a situation to feel … vulnerable. It's a fear I have every time I try to learn something new, like painting or writing a whole book! But you must overcome that fear with the belief that by learning more, you are setting yourself up for increased confidence. In fact, taking that leap to learn something new is itself a success! It is a down payment on an adventure you may make in the future.

It is far too easy to hold ourselves back from learning as we get older. The desire to learn is natural and we all do it, especially when we are young. We want to experience new things all the time. It's in our make-up to explore and seek knowledge. I've always been curious as to why that changes. *What makes us stop exploring? When do our minds become so comfortable with what we know that we don't want to change that?* When we are babies we teach ourselves to roll over, which leads to crawling, which leads to walking. The same thing happens with knowledge. Once you learn something, you want to learn something else and expand what you already know. In order to be a complete lifelong learner, you must learn to embrace the learning journey. You are never too old to learn and expand your knowledge. No matter where you are in your stage of life, there are opportunities every day, at every turn to learn something new. Embrace that moment. Cherish it. The key element to learning is possessing a positive and open minded attitude to accept, explore and live your new knowledge.

REFLECTIONS

Baby Boomer or not, what are you doing to serve others, so that not only do you spread your knowledge, but you learn too?

LAUGH

I often make the joke that my brain doesn't have a lot of space left, so in order to learn more I have to delete something. Of course this isn't true, but it does put a funny spin on learning. Remarkably up until twenty years ago, it was believed that your brain capacity was fully developed once infancy was over and thus we did have a limited capacity for knowledge. In Jonah Lehrer's book *Proust was a Neuroscientist*, he details the discovery of Elizabeth Gould, who in 1989, discovered that our brains never stop growing. She went on to discover that even if a child is born with diminished neurogenesis, through their act of living and exploration as a baby, their brains can develop back to normal capacity. The book says: "The mind is never beyond redemption, for no environment can extinguish neurogenesis. As long as we are alive, important parts of the brain are dividing."[4] Our brains are continually and endlessly supplied with new neurons which aids our learning, our lifelong learning. Continuing: "Since we each start every day with a slightly new brain, neurogenesis ensures that we our never done with our changes." (Pcont) Because we literally get a new brain each day, with a little more space to add new information, to grow what we already know or to challenge what is already stored, we are constantly changing. It's no wonder we sometimes wake up and smack ourselves on our foreheads because we thought of a brilliant new idea. Your brain actually grew while you slept to give you the freedom and capacity to discover new ideas!

You may not have the space to learn more today, but you definitely have the potential to learn it tomorrow. Life is a lot of repetitions and experiences and even if it takes you multiple attempts to learn something, eventually your brain will be ready for it.

I tried an experiment once while on a business trip. I had about an hour to kill so I trekked to a local mall to walk around. As I walked, I suddenly realized that I was moving along like most people I see, with my eyes fixed on the ground in front of me. Once I realized I had no reason to be walking with my head down, I heard the dance music pulsing from Abercrombie & Fitch. I immediately changed my attitude. I looked up. Not only that, I smiled as I walked. I looked at the people walking towards me and the ones sitting, relaxing. It wasn't a scientific test, but it was a sincere gesture of happiness. I believe that the more you smile, the more your brain will perceive a positive attitude. You are more apt to learn when you are in a positive frame of mind. My point here is simple: smile and don't take yourself too seriously. When you feel a smile or a laugh wanting to come bursting out of you – let it!

For example, if I tried to pick up a new hobby every day I would never be good at any of them! Painting is still a new hobby to me and it still provides me with stress sometimes. Recently, I finished a painting of Scottish tennis player Andy Murray. When I started I was excited about the potential of my creation – by the end I was embarrassed by the final product. It currently hangs in my hallway I walk down every day, with his larger-than-life body and his smaller-than-life head. I simply misjudged the canvas and ran out of room. I was mad in the immediate aftermath, but now when I walk by I smile and laugh at my work. I'm not perfect at painting, but I am definitely able to laugh at my successes and struggles and I try to learn a little something along the way as well. The key is to not focus on trying to learn all the time, but just have it be a part of your every day method. I truly believe that if people would laugh and enjoy life more, we would not only get better results in every facet of our lives, but we would learn more. If you're living life with a positive attitude and you know how to laugh at yourself, your mind and body is much more receptive to learning and new experiences.

When my boyfriend's sister, Daniela, finished her first day of kindergarten she bounded out to the car, excited to share what she had learned at her first day of school. "Today we learned the alphabet," she exclaimed. "Guess I don't have to go to school anymore. I've learned all there is to know." Even repeating the story, she laughs. Little did she know then that she was bound to become a doctor of veterinary medicine. Learning should be fun and, as I said earlier, you are going to fail and make mistakes. It is not fun for any of us to not succeed, but the success is in the journey, not the destination. Learning and growing is a continual, never-ending process.

Do you feel like all this talk about learning does not apply to you? Just because you are out of school and have no more exams and standardized tests to take, *does that mean you already know everything?* Back when I was in seventh grade at John Adams Middle School in Mr. Rood's Social Studies class, I saw I had a long way to go. Mr. Rood drew a square on the chalkboard. He said, "This box represents all the knowledge in the world." He then asked the smartest kid in the class to come up to the room and fill in the box with how much knowledge he felt he possessed.

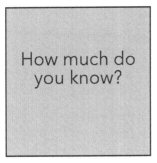

Our classmate marched to the chalkboard, taking the white, flaky chalk from our teacher. The square was probably about two-feet wide and my classmate filled in a rectangle that was nearly an inch thick. The entire class started to laugh. Mr. Rood was floored! His student was a genius! Mr. Rood then went to the board and went to the very corner of the same square and filled in a tiny speck of the corner. The exercise demonstrated how much knowledge remains for us to learn and explore. No matter how much of the box you filled in, I'm sure there is still some white space left to be filled up.

I remember that story because not only is it funny, it's true. We only know a percentage of a fraction of all the knowledge in this world. Each day there is more knowledge created and more knowledge for us to challenge. It is there for the taking – you just have to want it! In order to learn as much as you can, your mind must not only be open to learn, but you must possess the ability to laugh at yourself and the journey of knowledge discovery.

REFLECTIONS

What is one thing you want to learn about, since you now have open space?

How can you enjoy your life and laugh more?

from your knowledge bank. Tim Sanders writes in *Love is the Killer App*[5] that, "Our humanity can be defined as the ability to involved ourselves emotionally in the support of another person's growth." Sanders uses many examples to show how important sharing your knowledge and experiences with everyone around you is to your learning journey. He even says that for your knowledge to have any value at all, you must share it. Paraphrasing David Stern, the commissioner of the National Basketball Association since 1984, it is not completely important what people think about you – it is however, totally important how they feel about you. When you love to love others through the sharing of your knowledge, you leave a lasting impression that will stay with them forever.

This coincides with having passion in your life and shows how important it is to remain passionate in all you do, but certainly in the drive to love to learn. All of us are traveling on that infamous road less traveled and every step can be a lesson to share with someone who is on a completely different path than our own. You never know how or when you may be able to use a part of your life that was good or bad to positively touch someone. You may not even see it, but it happens all the time.

My favorite activity I do with my audiences is called *Life Lesson*. I ask everyone to sit silently and think for 60 or 90 seconds and come up with one lesson they have learned in their life they believe could be valuable to someone else and write it on a card. Then I have them share it with a partner and in turn ask them listen to someone else's lesson as well. It is always an incredible experience to see this play out and it always amazes me at the simple and powerful insight that ends up on those cards.

The first time I did this activity I felt like I was missing a great opportunity to continue the learning and expand it beyond just the one-on-one sharing. Now as part of this activity, I ask the audience to share with me their life lesson and supply me with their e-mail address. I collect them and select one a week to be included in an e-mail I send out to the hundreds who have already done this activity. This e-mail goes to people who want to be challenged and learn something new every week. If you're interested in signing up or submitting your lesson, see the back of the book for information for instructions on how to sign-up.

REFLECTIONS

So now, taking as much time as you want, come up with your Life Lesson:

I have been sharing the same lesson since I started leading workshops back in 2007.

> There are going to be great moments and tough challenges. There are going to be moments you'll never forget and moments you'll wish never happened. The truth is: being alive is being alive. It's a good thing.

My lesson is derived from multiple life experiences, both good and bad. But, and I say it again, *being alive is being alive. It's a good thing!* So long as I'm around, I'm going to do three things: Learn to learn. Learn to laugh. Learn to love. I try to do each every day. We must be lifelong learners in all three areas as each is dependent on the next. It is a continual challenge to be a lifelong learner. Constantly working out our brain and our emotions takes a lot of effort and energy, but through achieving this learning trifecta, you become a lifelong learner which is paramount to achieving your dreams.

Points to Remember

» If you assist others in their learning, you aid the learning journey of others and empower them to expand their knowledge.

» Be someone who shares your knowledge with the world.

» Listen to others because they may have information you don't have.

» You may not have the space to learn more information today, but you definitely have the potential to learn tomorrow.

» In order for learning to have any impact on your life, you have to love it.

» If you knowledge is going to have any value, you must share it with the world.

» The keys to being a lifelong learning are having a passion for learning, laughing at yourself and loving others enough to learn and share.

Chapter 9

Anything is Possible

"IF LIFE IS ONE LONG TO-DO LIST, I'M
GOING TO NEED A JUMBO-SIZED
YELLOW STICKY NOTE."

-Nick McCarvel

Do you believe it yet? It really is true. There are days I have to pinch myself to realize that, yes, anything really is possible! If I can do it, you can too! If Abraham Lincoln and Barack Obama and Jason McElwain and Ryan Borcherding can do it, you can to! There may appear to be things in your way, but nothing can keep your dreams from happening.

For me, the biggest obstacle to writing this book was me! The idea for this book had marinated for a long time. I devoted this entire book to changing your attitude so that no matter what, you can start believing that the "impossible" is really possible. Therefore, regardless of what stands before you, you can look at it and believe that yes, *I can do that.* It is not necessarily easy, but it is as simple as that.

As you read in *Chapter 5* in my *Life To Do List*, I wanted to write and publish a book. Well, here it is. I have achieved one of my life goals. I could say it was nothing, but I would be lying. It was hard work. It was painful. The editing took more time than I ever imagined. But it wasn't impossible. It was always possible. It was always my potential to achieve this dream. Now as it's done, I can say it, "It was nothing! Anything is possible!"

I have listened to the stories around me, finding hope and inspiration from each and every one of them. I hope you have too. When I think about what this book is about, it really boils down to one thing: You. This book is about what I believe you can accomplish and what you are hopefully beginning to believe as well. Now more than ever I believe that the sky's the limit. You are limited only by the limitations you impose upon yourself, real or imagined. *But the amazing thing is that even if you have a real-life limitation, who says you still can't do great things? When it comes down to it, who says you can't but yourself?* It comes down to you to stand up and believe that you *can*.

Carly Fiorina dropped out of law school at UCLA after her first semester. Slowly and incredibly she made her way to the summit of the business world. Her professional career began with various secretarial positions including one at Hewlett Packard and another at Marcus & Millichap. Finally in 1980, she was hired as a management trainee with AT&T and attended the prestigious MIT Sloan School of Management under the Sloan Fellows program in 1989. From the time she was hired in 1980, she catapulted up the corporate ladder, all the way to Group President of Lucent in 1997. In fact, in 1998, Fiorina was named the most powerful woman in business. It is a title she held until 2004.

After 15 years at AT&T and Lucent, Fiorina was offered a new position to become the CEO of Hewlett Packard. She joined just before the burst of the dot-com bubble. As she navigated the company through the downturn, she saw an opportunity to expand their reach into some of their weaker markets. It is well known that she was a proponent of the merger between HP and Compaq, despite high levels of criticism and planning. In her book, *Tough Choices*, Fiorina continues to stand by that daring and monumental decision. In the end the Board ultimately didn't see it as a positive step. With a lack of growth three years after the merger, Fiorina was released as CEO.

The key element to take from her story is not that she was fired, but that in 1980 she was a law school dropout working temp jobs and twenty years later she earned recognition as one of the 30 most powerful women in America by *Forbes Magazine*. Not only that, but she believed so strongly that the merger was the correct move for the company, she stood behind it and didn't back down. While she lost her position at HP over the decision, she has gone on to great things. Did she think it was impossible to work her way up back in 1980? Maybe, but through her previous experiences, she knows that she can achieve anything she puts her mind to.

In December 2008, I joined Twitter, the online micro-blogging site with no clear purpose or understanding of the service. A year later, I now use it to share what I'm doing at any given moment, promote books, movies, blog postings, new ideas, events, music and my other many interests. I also utilize it to pose questions to my followers. It's a fun adventure that five years ago I would not have imagined possible. The other thing I do on Twitter is "follow" people with similar interests. It's beyond cool to see how they live their lives and what moments in their life are important enough to share and to find out what articles they are reading. It's just one more avenue for me to learn and share. One small glimmer of knowledge can spread out to hundreds of people and create an enormous impact. Every time we learn we help ourselves, but we also have an unlimited potential to touch others when we share our knowledge. Always seeking new information and then surrounding yourself with those that have it is a crucial element to personal and professional success. Despite its 140 character limit for each "tweet", I have also found Twitter to be astoundingly powerful. No challenge is too great for our interconnected world.

In April 2008, photojournalist James Karl Buck helped free himself from an Egyptian jail with a one-word blog post from his cell phone.[1] After being arrested by local authorities in Mahalla, Egypt, Buck sent a message using Twitter that was enough to cause a storm of alarm back home amongst his friends. On his way to the police station, Buck took out his cell phone with time only to send a single one-word tweet, "Arrested." He was later released and is still working with his Twitter connections to find his friend who was also detained at the same time. Did Twitter aid his release ... no one can say for certain, but maybe it helped.

An even more powerful story occurred in January 2009. Although it didn't get a lot of news coverage, I found it amazing because I happened to be following it live on my Twitter feed. One of the people I follow is David Armano (@Armano). David is currently senior vice president at Edelman Digital. He tweeted one evening that read, "Hey everyone. I am going to need a very BIG favor from you. It's going to be asking a lot. I'll let you know more very soon." That was all. Then an hour later, he posted about the need for donations to aid someone he and his wife had taken in from an abusive husband. What happened with his network of 8,150 followers is nothing short of amazing. Armano's announced goal was to raise $5,000 to help the woman and her kids get on their feet. In less than 48 hours, he raised a staggering $16,880.60. Other than the time it took Armano to build this network, it took a small effort on the part of everyone involved and ultimately changed the lives of Daniela and her children.[2]

We all have the ability to take simple actions like that. We can change the world. We can affect one person.

REFLECTIONS

You have already answered the question in Chapter 2, but what "impossible" in your life will you now make possible?

How? What will you change? What will you challenge about yourself? What will you dare yourself to do?

Now regarded as an inspiring entrepreneur, David W. Anderson wasn't always the leader he is today. His website reads, "Always tackling the impossible, this bottom half of the class high school student has earned his Master's Degree from Harvard University without an undergraduate degree!"[3] You may not know him, so let me help: Anderson is the founder of *Famous Dave's of America*, the warm and welcoming BBQ franchise with over 120 locations. He also helped create the *Rainforest Café*, another successful and well-known restaurant. In addition, he played an integral role in the founding of three publically traded companies and assisted in creation of over 20,000 jobs. His biography reads like an inspiring tale – and it is. Anderson even served two U.S. Presidents and three governors in advisory roles, including the Assistant Secretary – Indian Affairs in the Department of the Interior. I'm willing to bet that as a child he never dreamed he would accomplish all that he has. I would place even more money on a bet that he is only getting started. He has had his hurdles just like you and I. Prior to his success, Anderson lived a financially stressful life, ridden with bankruptcy. I imagine during those years, the idea of success was a lofty, impossible idea. Now he is well-known and respected, living the impossible dream. He believed what I have been saying all along: anything is possible.

Years ago while working at *The Lighthouse*, a local bookstore, I remember the book *A Child Called "It"*. I'd heard comments about it through the media and a friend of mine had recommended it to me so I read it over the course of just a few days. The author, Dave Pelzer embodies the notion that tough times don't last, tough people do. Pelzer was abused as a child. Not just abused, but tortured. Some people tried to help, but nothing could stop the abuse. His mother called him not by his birth name but a new name label: *It*.

Pelzer describes the various tactics his mother used to abuse him, from forcing ammonia down his throat, making him sit in a "gas chamber", physically abusing him and "accidentally" stabbing him when he didn't meet the time limit to do the dishes. Repeatedly throughout the book he talks about how he thought he was going to die and how much better it would be than living. But then after one incident when he came close to death, he survived, and a new sense of purpose and hope enveloped him. He realized he could come out of his situation alive. He could save his life. About two months after his 12th birthday, on March 5, 1973, Pelzer was rescued by teachers at his school. As reported in the San Francisco Chronicle, schoolteacher Athena Konstan of Salt Lake City wrote, "In my 31 years of teaching, David Pelzer was the most severely abused child I have ever known."[4] Pelzer kept his hope alive and now he had a true reason to believe. His belief didn't start with his rescue; it started with his realization earlier that he could survive his mother. Now with his rescue, he was completely free to live. To him, the impossible was living a normal, happy life. For most of us, living a normal and happy life is almost a normal and average thought. That can give each of us hope, that because our own impossibilities are maybe somebody else's normal which means impossible actually isn't.

It doesn't matter if the obstacle is only yours or if it is a whole team challenge. You and everyone around you must buy-in and believe the challenge is possible to overcome. With just a single person, it is harder to find the inspiration to believe it, but not impossible. With a team, once one person starts to believe, it can become infectious.

In 1980, the United States faced the worst economic times since the end of World War II. There were gas lines and an energy crisis along with double-digit inflation. The Cold War was as cold as ever and amidst it all, the Winter Olympics were upon us. For 20 years the U.S.S.R. hockey team had been untouchable and unbeatable, winning Olympic gold medals in 1964, '68, '72 and '76. No one anticipated these games would be any different. For a year leading up to the Games, a group of nearly thiry players and coaches practiced and studied like their lives depended on it. They were the team that would later become known as the "Miracle on Ice." Much has been made of this team, including a Disney movie, "Miracle."

If you don't know the rest of the story, as a team of amateurs they had little chance of getting into the medal round, much less winning the gold medal. On February 9, a week before the Games were to begin, the United States squad faced the Soviet Union team in an exhibition game. The Soviet Union unsurprisingly won handily, 10-3. After this game, it seemed unlikely the United States team would win a medal. It had just been proven they were nothing against the greatest hockey team in the world.

One day before the U.S. and the Soviets were set to meet in the medal round, Dave Anderson, a New York Times columnist, wrote, "unless the ice melts, or unless the United States team or another team performs a miracle, as did the American squad in 1960, the Russians are expected to easily win the Olympic gold medal for the sixth time in the last seven tournaments."[5] The U.S. team faced off against the Soviet Union in what would decide who would play in gold medal game. For months leading up to the Games, the U.S. squad worked harder than any U.S. squad before them. Coach Herb Brooks is said to have run the toughest training camp any hockey coach had seen up to that point. The U.S. team battled for 60 intense minutes, skating hard, hitting harder, and wanting it and believing it more as each minute ticked off the clock. The rest, they say, is history. "Eleven seconds. You've got ten seconds. The countdown going on right now! Morrow, up to Silk. Five seconds left in the game. Do you believe in miracles? Yes!" Al Michaels shouted as he called out the winning moment. The Americans defeated the unbeatable team and went on to win the Olympic gold medal. A year before the game, winning any medal was an impossible dream, but they still dared to chase it and believe it. They overcame every obstacle, real and imagined, to reach the pinnacle of their sport. They believed in the possible and they now have an Olympic gold to prove it.

The extraordinary events that unfolded for those two weeks in Lake Placid live on and represent the power of a true belief in the impossible. Every time I watch the movie or read about that game and those players, I get chills down my spine. They are the embodiment of what this book is all about. Not only were they up against a titanic opponent, they were up against their own doubts. Writer Wayne Coffey sums it up best, "The naïveté spawned a boldness to shoot for a completely far-fetched goal. You never know if you never try."[6]

One of my favorite bands is Switchfoot. Anytime I need inspiration, motivation, a quick pick-me-up, or I just want to smile, without fail I just need to play Switchfoot. I'm fascinated by their music. I have listened to their songs dozens of times and they still move me. Their sound is melodic, moody, emotional and touches my soul every time the words hit me. That's how Jon Foreman, the leader of the band creates the music; he uses music to question things that are on his mind and explore the answers. Their name even shares who they are. "Switchfoot" is a surfing term meaning to switch your stance to face the opposite direction. Foreman says it's about "change and movement, a different way of approaching life and music."[7] Maybe that's why I love their music so much. Their lyrics speak to me, pushing me to believe in tomorrow. To believe in the impossible is to believe in your potential. You must believe that no matter what your circumstances, your obstacles, your challenges, past experiences, failures, victories, fears, worries and trepidations, you can do it. Our lives are full of questions which can sometimes take a lifetime to answer. But you must question your life in order to find the answers to your dreams. You may have to change your course, change your tactics, reevaluate your goals and you may have to switchfoot, but you can achieve anything.

My favorite Switchfoot song is called "Awakening." Their lyrics speak to what this book is truly about:[8]

> Maybe it's called ambition, you've been talking in your sleep
> About a dream, we're awakening
> Last week found me living for nothing but deadlines,
> With my dead beat day but, this town doesn't look the same
>   tonight
> These dreams started singing to me out of nowhere
> And in all my life I don't know that I ever felt so alive,
> Alive

As I finish this book, I hope you take a few things with you:

First, I hope that you can use the stories and examples in this book to help you believe that all things are possible. Through these stories you can see that no matter the challenge, it is possible to change your attitude and ultimately, your life.

Second, I trust you have spent some time in thought as you have gone through the questions posed to begin sketching your *Life To Do List*. This book can be a guide for you. I never intended this to be a "how-to" book, but rather one to inspire you to simply believe in the potential of every moment and every obstacle. Oftentimes, that's all we have in this life: a simple, bottom-line, unquenchable belief that all things are possible. I encourage you to bookmark some of the lists or questions you have entered in here and keep them handy for moments when you need encouragement or motivation from your own life. Your journey is just beginning.

Finally, I hope you are ready to live. It's up to you now. It's up to you to begin changing your life. No matter how big or how small, I trust you to do it. I trust you to start climbing the mountain to see what's on the other side. I believe you can do great things in your life. I believe even the smallest changes can amount to untold riches. I truly believe that for you, anything is possible, and I know without a shred of doubt that you can believe it too.

Examine where you are right now and where you want to be.

Eliminate the word "not" from your vocabulary because there is nothing you cannot do.

Maintain a positive attitude in everything that you do.

Live the life that you truly want.

Try anything and everything. Seek out and welcome new experiences.

Overcome the obstacles in your life. Know that usually you are your own biggest obstacle.

Chase your true passion without hesitation or fear.

Commit yourself to a lifetime of learning, laughing and loving.

I end with a quote from a personal journal of one of my best friends. For the last two years he's been by my side through thick and thin and pushed me to achieve my dreams and to believe in the impossible:

> Never give up. Never stop. Stay true to who you are. Change. Love is always worth it. Live a life of freedom. Seek truth. Discover beauty. That's all I have to say about that. The rest I will just live.

Go live your life. Believe it: Anything is Possible!

Acknowledgments

I wrote down the idea for this book nearly five years ago. I wrote it down with the dream I would one day bring the idea full-circle into a book. This is the completion of that vision.

I owe a great deal of thanks to the many people who have helped and advised me with this project along the way. First and foremost must be Asitha Jayawardena. He offered my first inspiration and has been the best friend the world has to offer. He is the true embodiment of *Anything is Possible*.

I would be remiss if I didn't acknowledge Evan Zach, Andrew Flusche, Tricia Olson and Eric Coborn who provided legal advice throughout the journey. Also, fellow authors Chris Amisano and Sean Nickell provided priceless insight into the editing and publishing process.

Since I finished my first draft of this book nearly a year ago, my volunteer editors, Karith Humpal and Stephen Barnes, have put in countless hours and have offered me advice too many times to count. Justin Brady reviewed my early notes and helped me flesh out ideas into their current form. Their involvement in this project only made it stronger.

I must also thank everyone who believed in me before I believed in myself. The journey hasn't been easy, but each day I seek to live my life with an attitude that anything is possible.

Finally, my never-ending thanks and gratitude must go to my most ardent supporter, Nathanael Porembka. He quite possibly put more energy into this project than me. He kept me going on the late nights when I had hundreds of edits and too little coffee. He is the one who first pushed me to chase after my dreams and I will always be indebted to him for that. He is my friend, my sounding board and the most amazing boyfriend I could ever ask for.

Ultimately, this is for you. I want you to believe and live a life in which anything is possible. That could quite possibly be my greatest achievement.

Richard Dedor
December 2009

Bibliography

Chapter 1

1. Hyatt, M. (2007, March 6). *The Quarterly Review.* Retrieved November 14, 2009, from Michael Hyatt: http://michaelhyatt.com/2007/03/the-quarterly-review.html

2. Davidson, S. (2009, February 10). *Why I Gave Up Trying to Balance Work and Life and Decided to Stay Sane Instead.* Retrieved October 12, 2009, from Sam Davidson: http://samdavidson.blogspot.com/2009/02/why-i-gave-up-trying-to-balance-work.html

Chapter 2

1. Sorin, R. (2003). Research with children: a rich glimpse into the world of childhood. *Australian Journal of Early Childhood, 28* (1), 31-35.

2. *Summary Data for Barack Obama.* (2008, December 31). Retrieved December 13, 2009, from OpenSecrets: http://www.opensecrets.org/pres08/summary.php?id=n00009638

Chapter 4

1. *Our Story.* (n.d.). Retrieved December 9, 2009, from The V Foundation: http://www.jimmyv.org/about-us.html

2. (n.d.). Retrieved September 22, 2009, from Challenged Athletes Foundation: http://www.challengedathletes.org/about_caf/

Chapter 6

1. *Cancer Facts and Figures 2008.* (n.d.). Retrieved December 10, 2009, from American Cancer Society: http://www.cancer.org/downloads/STT/2008CAFFfinalsecured.pdf

2. (2007). Retrieved December 1, 2009, from World Health Organization: http://data.unaids.org/pub/EPISlides/2007/2007_epiupdate_en.pdf

3. King JT, J. A. (2003). Long-term HIV/AIDS survival estimation in the highly active antiretroviral therapy era. *Medical Decision Making*, 9-20.

Chapter 7

1. *Pennsylvania Artist Mark Beekman Creates World's Largest Lite-Brite.* (2007, July 7). Retrieved October 12, 2009, from News Blaze: http://newsblaze.com/story/2007071107010200001.ew/topstory.html

2. Drehs, W. (2006, June 14). *J-Mac's meaningful message for autism.* Retrieved September 16, 2009, from ESPN: http://sports.espn.go.com/espn/news/story?id=2352763

3. *The Heiligenstadt Testimony.* (n.d.). Retrieved December 14, 2009, from Ludwig van Beethoven: http://www.lvbeethoven.com/Bio/BiographyHeiligenstadtTestament.html

Chapter 8

1. StateMaster. (2009). *StateMaster - Encyclopedia: B. F. Skinner.* Retrieved November 16, 2009, from StateMaster: http://www.statemaster.com/encyclopedia/B.-F.-Skinner

2. Evans, O. (1989, December 7). *In France A College For Elderly Students.* Retrieved November 16, 2009, from The New York Times: http://www.nytimes.com/1989/12/07/garden/in-france-a-college-for-elderly-students.html

3. Kanter, R.M. (2006, July & August). *Back to College.* Retrieved November 3, 2009, from AARP The Magazine: http://w w w .aarpmagazine.org/lifestyle/back_to_college.html

4. Lehrer, J. (2007) *Proust Was a Neuroscientist.* New York: Houghton Mifflin Harcourt.

5. Sanders, T. (2002) *Love is the Killer App.* New York: Three Rivers Press.

Chapter 9

1. Simon, M. (2008, April 25). *Student 'Twitters' his way out of Egyptian jail.* Retrieved November 10, 2009, from CNN.com: http://www. cnn.com/2008/TECH/04/25/twitter.buck/

2. Armano, D. (2009, January 6). *Please Help Us Help Daniela's Family.* Retrieved August 10, 2009, from Logic+Emotion: http:// darmano.typepad.com/logic_emotion/2009/01/pleas-help-us-help-daniellas-family.html

3. (n.d.). Retrieved October 18, 2009, from David W. Anderson: http://www.davidwanderson.com/bio2.html

4. Carroll, J. (1998, July 15). The Beaten Path: Author David Pelzer chronicles a nightmare childhood. *San Francisco Chronicle.*

5. Open-Mic: Greatest Sports Achievement--Do You Believe in Miracles? (n.d.). Retrieved December 14, 2009, from Bleacher Report:http://bleacherreport.com/articles/28926-open-mic-greatest-sports-achievements-do-you-believe-in-miracles

6. Coffey, W. (2006). *The Boys of Winter.* New York: Three Rivers Press.

7. *Interview: Switchfoot.* (2000, August 25). Retrieved May 10, 2009, from Jesusfreakhideout.com: http://www.jesusfreakhideout.com/ interviews/Switchfoot.asp

8. Switchfoot (Performer). (2006). Awakening. On *Oh! Gravity.*

FOCUS
The Weekly Life Lesson

You have learned something in your life that someone else can learn something from as well. This Weekly Lesson is how those lessons are shared and touch hundreds of people around you.

Upon signing up you will receive the weekly *FOCUS: The Weekly Life Lesson* e-mail, which includes a weekly lesson and inspirational thoughts on how that lesson can apply to your life, today. It takes fewer than 60 seconds to read and that's it. No sales pitches and no spam, just the weekly Lesson.

This is a simple way for you to impact the lives of people around you and listen to the lessons of others.

Visit *www.richarddedor.com* and click "sign up" to start getting the e-mails today. I would love to hear what your Life Lesson is – you may submit it to me by emailing *focusonyou@richarddedor.com* or via the website.

Change your life one lesson at a time.

-Richard

About the Author

A national motivational speaker, personal coach and author, writing is just one way Richard Dedor devotes his time to changing the world. Richard's work has appeared in *Sports 'n Spokes* magazine and the *Liberty Press*. He is also a contributor to *Primer Mag* and has been an editor with a regional non-profit publication, all the while presenting his motivational messages. His experiences in the non-profit sector and in politics as a candidate for mayor of Mason City, Iowa, have given him a wealth of experience that provides constant inspiration.

Richard holds a degree in public relations from the University of Northern Iowa and was a 2002 recipient of the Iowa Bar Association's American Citizenship Medal. This book is the first of a new journey.

Richard can be found and contacted online at the following sites:

richarddedor.com
richarddedor.com/blog
twitter.com/richarddedor
facebook.com/richarddedor
linkedin.com/in/richarddedor

Made in the USA
Charleston, SC
25 January 2010